AMERICA ALIENATION NATION ALIENATION MACHINATION POETRY

Author

Edward R. Ingram BA, MA Credentialed Teacher

Dorrance Publishing Co
585 Alpha Drive, Suite 103
Pittsburgh, PA 15238
Visit our website at *www.dorrancebookstore.com*

ISBN: 979-8-8852-7046-5
eISBN: 979-8-8852-7775-4

FOREWORD

This book is divided into chapters spelling out the stages of emotional development as government institutions proved detrimental to the people suffering through four years of a self-serving administration bent on personal acquisition of wealth and power willing to let Americans die to get it. As the actions first invoke mistrust, I found myself going through stages of emotional rift as disgust, then shock, anger, frustration, stability must be achieved as resolve, focus, dedication, solution, resolution can be a means to gather inner strength, turn and face the menace. This book can highlight a primary feature repeated in several treatise the condition of "if existence," a determination of reality judgmental in question of fact. Is any life in conjunction with a modern colonized world really a true physical social real-time event worthwhile in the elemental sense, kindred safe compatible progressive, or is it deplorable alienation machination abomination we continue to endeavor to persevere just to survive humanity groveling in the mud and swamp? What? How? When? Why? Questions poignant in consideration of the machination of alienation tactical oppression targeting specific society and culture with influential results stimulus causally related to continuing escalating turmoil conflicts endangering certain communities and civilians impacting lives negatively.

I must and will consider myself lucky to both write and publish. I have designed this book to be a modern presentation unlike most reads. I could not help myself in the last six months of the Trump presidency. I awoke daily alarmed, disgusted in so much disbelief of the bleak future ahead if this were to continue that I could not help myself. I am not a talkative person, of course among certain friends I talk way too much but I used my cellphone daily to text family and friends daily after watching news of the morning. I got lots of cool responses so I continued which acted to provide some solace. I have not had intentions to write a book or novel, I am formerly acquainted with author Walter Mosely, his *Easy Rollins* mysteries have been made into movies. He also exposed me to reading *Tom Swift* novels, some of which I still remember. This book wrote itself, really my inability to stop texting continued for months, thus a lot of things were said. To provide them for this book I am going to present it to you in largely a text format important to the reader because I could never duplicate what was said without having record of it. I have written this book with kindred intentions, I must admit in some areas there will be negative contents and comments about brutal actions yielded by a presidency not for the people, also I will be honest and direct in my compositions and criticisms my intent reactionary as never before have I witnessed such a poor combination Trump and presidency. I will also venture into areas not of my expertise with critical issues facing Americans some will criticize, make negative judgments, call me silly or mental as I make discussions of a different path to outer space exploration. To criticize me is to express same for Isaac Asimov, Ray Bradbury, Aldous Huxley, Robert Heinlein, as they dared to express theoretical ideology, I am in good company. This will not be an easy read but I try to use humor throughout. I believe in being merciful, this personal quality is rare. Something to keep in mind like food for thought, the Billionaire Space Race is cute, opulence feel good moments about the future of civilian participation in space exploration and recreation but the collection of recovered vehicles used by other civilizations to cross time and space to arrive here are not anything like rockets.

I am lucky to have survived to write this foreword, a black male in these United States. My awareness begins at 3 years old as largely confusion as attention and behavior develop through gestures and language development. I lived with my Aunt Mae and Uncle Jack Castleman, fortunate my father's sister lived close enough to influence and in fact start me down the path to learning later to rescue me from myself and the terrors of war even paving the way as the determined homeowners to freedom for others truly saintly and remarkable, more of this later. My mother was born in Richmond, VA, my father born in Conyers, GA, so there was lot of rich country elegance in my city boy upbringing living in Los Angeles leaving Queens, New York, behind. The story of life with my parents and my one younger brother Vernon Jon is as tragic as losing my sister at birth especially to this day I do not know my nieces or nephews, I am the second born to Edward and Lottie. I will spare you the details of what can only be described as a great start but the stress of war, broken dreams, economic hardship led to abuse which mounted with every year. Finally realization Lottie was abusing me and my brother over not being able to control her husband eventually using me to coax my dad to not spend all his money in the bar before paying the rent. One day I tried to seek outside help as schools were supposed to be nurturing places, I talked with a teacher and a counselor told them of our abusive mother and stated our lives are in danger. They did not listen to me or believe me so I ran from them, it took 4 hours of a chase on elementary school ground with the police involved at the end of which they gave me right back to my murderous abusive mother. I was nearly killed not being able to meet her needs. Ultimately, I formed a pact with my younger brother, I would take the responsibility as the oldest to kill my mother if our lives became threatened in self-defense. After having approached my dad urgently to deal with the abuse only to wind up attacked while asleep in bed by a hysterical wife stressed-out temporarily insane woman hitting me over the head repeatedly with a spiked high-heel shoe placing about 15 holes in my head. She hid me in the bathroom when my father came in drunk, wrapped in the blood-soaked bedsheet and threatened me not to speak as my dad stumbled into his room, closed the door and left his battered son to the vicious perpetrator while my younger brother still slept. The following Monday I went to school, partway through a class a student tapped me quietly on the shoulder to let me know I was bleeding down the back of my neck, this was high school. I was just one of the lucky ones to survive my mother. Shortly after the horror just described a young high school girl I had known for almost three years because of the location of our lockers came to me one day greatly distressed, said she had a gun, showed it to me and said she wanted to kill herself. I heard the tardy bell and instead of staying by her side I told her I was going to class but would not tell anyone and would try to help her in any way after school obligation. I regret that decision as long as I live, students throughout my high school heard the report a gunshot that killed her. She then shot herself on a front lawn across the street. Students could see her lifeless body from the school windows. After high school graduation time spent getting to know a new family as I was lucky a white friend provided me the shelter and wisdom provided by his family I can never forget, Bryan, Chris, Doug, Ray, Tita, and Alex Caldwell Sr., guidance much needed as experimentation became a way of life and time spent undecided needing to find myself. I am leaving a lot of great stories of my childhood and adolescence out, they became dimmed by the brutality of my mother only to find it more widespread being on the receiving end of white boy justice undeserved as he lashed out at me but I was not the cause of his anger, he hurled a fist-sized rock at me hitting me in the back of the head, leaving a ½-inch gash in my skull gushing blood as I scrambled for my bike to escape his furious volley. I resolved then I would kill that white boy if I ever got the chance, I was twelve years old at the time. I left my home at sixteen, luckily my aunt and uncle provided useful guidance including shelter but after failed attempt at college education I became too fond of alcohol and drugs, wound up homeless sleeping in a 1965 Pontiac Lemans. When folks passed I gave up drinking and smoking cigarettes, set out working and became a workaholic. This is the result of time to recover from a brutal attack by a Los Angeles police officer. In 1976 before breaking into construction advanced my working years I spent time exploring creativity to write music and dabble at mechanical design engineering. I was saddened at the loss of firefighters battling a raging fire in the Los Angeles Santa Monica mountains, and immediately designed a lifesaver device to rescue a firefighter in/from a firestorm. A device when activated and deployed provides immediate shelter from a blazing fire, keeps firefighters cool and uses an external chemical retardant to lessen the fire threat, shelter can last up to 90 minutes. The first model was improved in 1984 as reusable, can be carried to the front lines or stably mounted on a truck or in a building to save lives. The night I completed the first device in June I think or July, I went to a friend's house to talk technical issues related to device deployment. My friend just home from work needed beer, afraid to go two blocks to a store I went and found out why he had been unwilling. I was stopped by LA. police officers S.R. Tims and his partner in the Pacific Division for no apparent reason. I complied to get out of the car with my license. I was immediately handcuffed, placed in a bar arm control lock, lifted off the ground and with his knee in my back he tried to strangle me until I almost passed out. Being 24 at the time in extremely good physical condition I tightened my neck, he could not get me to lose consciousness, lowered me to the ground then stepped on my face, grinding my teeth into the ground and said, "Now nigger do something." Being in shock, it took me time to recover but at the station when the officers exited the vehicle I made my best effort to kick the windows out of the car. One of the officers hurt his leg moving so quickly when he heard me get down. I was then charged with Battery on a Police Officer, though never battered the officer. I was beaten brutally, accused, falsely charged and convicted to serve a sentence though innocent of the act. I have no greater desire than to beat S. R. Tims to death even now in 2021-2022. The naked truth, you can be a true saint, an angel, a wonderful human being on earth with only the best intentions, but there is evil here entrenched in profit-making enterprises that stoke its flames in every location, you cannot avoid it, you will be victimized by it more than once. Some do not survive its encounter, those that do await the next more keen on survival against a timeless unseen enemy that daily can and does change lives, using this knowledge protect yourselves, our futures remain in constant jeopardy.

Spent years driving a cab and a tow truck, worked as a carpenter, plumber, electrical, gardening, landscaping, tree planting and removal, truck driver all while sleeping and living out of my 1965 Pontiac Lemans I rebuilt while working at Boggs and McBurney Auto Parts in West LA and Santa Monica, then got smart, went back to college and made it real. To go back to college at age 35 was a necessary path to education and a job provided by the State of California General Relief and a deal I made with Venice Yard Supervisors allowed me to work weekends and complete years of undergraduate studies at UCSB, CSN, Valley college, Pearce college, CSUN work on weekdays. Eventually, going back to college completing graduate courses at UCLA graduating CSUN earning a BA, MA, Teaching Credentials and numerous Authorizations, taught for eighteen years English and History with

LAUSD before retiring. It is in graduate school that I was approached by a teaching professional to apply for the teaching job I held for eighteen years. During one of those years a wonderful moment in my life came while eating free Skakey's Pizza and drinking beer. While talking to a lawyer that represents teachers I found that Mae and Jack Castleman versus the City of Palm Springs, my aunt and uncle won a case for minorities to buy homes setting permanent state, local and federal precedent for perpetuity, may they Rest in Peace. Now retired from teaching but reentered the world of construction having some accumulated fifty years in the field. Trying to do all the right things to stay alive and live a healthy path of love and wellness with my wife, an angel here on earth. I was forced to retire from LAUSD after 18 years, wanting to go at least twenty-five years. Ironically LAUSD took advantage of teachers when they declared an Emergency and reduced teacher salaries without promise of reinstated salaries felt to be punitive though stated the contrary. State of CA joined in and also reduced salaries overall, reduced salaries by 18%, my salary went from 96 thousand per year to 78 thousand with same expectation of faithful service and dedication. I was in the process of receiving what would have been my last raise to put my salary over 100,000 per year, a lifelong working goal in progress. In addition, they used a lie, one white principal stated a lie, he said, "I hit a student with a chair," that was enough to destroy a career teacher with a near perfect teaching history. So from the start of my white-collar career in teaching where as a new teacher I was stabbed in the back by a black female colleague that manipulated schedules to take my teaching partner years, later I witnessed major tragedy in her life. I still dedicated myself to professional excellence serving parents, students, school and community only to be thrown under the bus by a white principal with two strikes over sexual misconduct with the district who then used a lie to end my contract. The termination process was a brutal two-year torture termed "Teacher Jail," what a pleasure it must have been for the entire white termination staff to place a qualified innocent professional black teacher colleague in jail at home, denied any contact with the school, they rubbed my nose in guilt for nothing, embarrassed me in front of students and coworkers. I find their actions irresponsible and reprehensible. I find their actions suspect and criminal, taking earned salaries away without promise of reinstatement. I see this agency as an organization of thugs much like the police without weapons. However, there are valuable teachers doing amazing things in their employment.

Then the horror Donald Trump was elected, it was similar to Hitler's election outcome in Germany years before. The day the people became damned, tortured, killed outright, four years of intolerable atrocities. So it began the most heinous, vicious, cruel, incomprehensible, sadistic, violent, racist wannabe autocratic regime, abused America, Americans and our Allies.

CONTENTS

Foreword v

Mistrust 1

Disgust...7

Shock 13

Anger 17

Frustration..19

Resolve..27

Focus..59

Dedication 79

Resolution 123

Musical Construct 135

Epilogue 159

MISTRUST

The impact of shock wearing off was not soo damaging, as I knew it was possible Trump would win the election. Now trying to plan for the future when it seemed from the moment he took office things radically changed. It became immediately apparent trust would be an issue with the new administration. The new president started raging about his inauguration was the biggest in history, it obviously was not but for months this stupid lying crap went on. The people surrounding him including his chief of staff seemed subordinated by his vanity and bald-face lies. Thus so began the pattern of bending, twisting, concealing, altering, pining, inflating, molding, the truth to fit the needs of an unrepresentative administrative government. After nearly four years of the most dastardly presidency ever, I could no longer keep quiet about the presidential abusive beast, after all anyone or administration that would separate children from their parents possibly never to be reunited is beyond a human monster. These and other heinous acts continued throughout this miserable presidency. Our very citizenry was under daily assault from presidential Tweets that were gross to witness much less comprehend. The new administration displayed altered states as if representing people from another universe, one filled with fantasy and a lot of bullshit. My mistrust of the new administration was manifest in my need to break my normal silence and make contact with friends and family and speak daily to understand that I was not alone, viewing this presidency as an enigma this nation did not need and will never recover from. I did this by texting often early in the morning at first, just a few words evolved daily to reveal, analyze, question, fact check the administration and its bullies, making a mockery of our democracy, disrespecting our allies worldwide, causing a stuuupid Trade War with China compromising our American farmers. I had to respond to the alienation I now felt more than ever. So it started, as I listen to the articles covered in morning news stories about efforts to get into colleges and the increases in fraud and corruption to get in. Year after year of the same old with not enough discussion about what's really going on, racism backlash as efforts continue to deny access for POC alienation is the compound complex result. Lifelong stigma relevant to perverse prejudices to prevent dignified lifestyles. Alienation is the behemoth every place, everywhere, everyone so common tolerated and yet rarely discussed in explicit terms. Continuing to grow constantly as racial confrontations produce some progressive results, white racist backlash is the byproduct of alienation, the spike driven into the soul of a nation and its people meant to be permanent inescapable. White America imposes alienation on all non-white and those who sympathize with POC, a consequence of existence in this extreme of deranged perverted aspersions to enslave and deny. Caught a glimpse of American treachery in Looney Tunes characters as racist prejudices, common knowledge were occasionally seen as a part of cartoon madness, remember the shrunken Daffy Duck races to hug a large jewel saying, "I'm a happy miser!" The carrot dangled for the mass's potential to gather wealth continues to power drive to succeed. Success here is always marred by hatred, racism, backlash, contempt, thus alienation, leading to necessity, creates complex structures to tolerate the intolerable.

The ultimate white power profiting from the Machination of Alienation gaining wealth, power, more privilege at all times, especially during war or pandemic crisis. If Trump wins the election the truth is revealed about this atrociously apologetic fallibly responsible nation having purposely plied the result of human relocation to cause this systemic dysfunctional variation racism generating a side-effect supremism, permanently damaging the psycho cohesion of the sociopolitical fabric of a modern society. His their victory will be nothin' but much, much, much more of the same. No less than a damn shame.

Food for thought. At a super-spreader Trump rally successful African-American entrepreneur Herman Kane was in attendance second row behind speaker Trump. Interestingly odd coincidence, Kane caught, suffered and died from COVID-19 so quickly after this event. Could he have been targeted for infection for some deranged reason? After all, Trump uses his victims before discarding them. Was Kane no longer useful, preferring Kanye West instead an easier mark?

The underlying tragedy exposed by the heinous actions of a wealthy, powerful, orange-white megalomanic attacking our democracy, he was able to use the medium of TV press rallies Tweets to instigate insurrection by convincing feeble-minded incompetents to violently try to stop transition of power foolhardy insular, an impossible pipe dream causing the masses to act as a murderous mob, revealing the original reason for the formation of the Electoral College, a Framer's consideration of frivolous became the reason we are denied our majority freedom to this very day. Classically ironic as half our population are bent on dragging the rest of us all to their hell on earth. Uniquely embarrassing to those cultivated with a sense of clear and straight-thinking progressive nonviolent seeking a path to modernity without danger or intimidation. To prove those old white pioneers right that the public is potentially a danger to itself is an ugly, sad statement of the human condition. Now more than ever our nation is more of a vicious prison than confinement being formally incarcerated. Since earliest contact with colonizers indigenous were doomed no matter what acceptance to be removed left out the means of production off-limits Infinitum. Machination started with the earliest exposure to Anglo cultures and evolves, mutates, bends, flexes but works to constantly manipulate the manner in which immigration and assimilation even when acculturation is mostly demeaning, detrimental to equality manipulating lifestyles primarily for people of color. Machination is systemic institutionalized, profitable greed driven motivated by wealth and power. Those of us who earn our living legally often don't thrive as well as successful drug dealers or gun runners or exploitive industries, sports, entertainment, movies, video gaming, gambling, selling explosives, clean living is genuine. Everything around us everywhere you look, media advertising, executive jobs, opportunity industry molded by white entrepreneurship to advance racial partnerships entrenched in businesses that do not believe in trickle-down, more like putting people down. Millions deal with the horrendous effects of years of developmental machination daily as a matter of routine. It is to the point of grotesque criminalism contrary to Democratic values but exerts lots of control over the course of our lives. Machination of alienation is unwanted manipulation and control existing for eons with no plans to weaken in the immediate future a compliment of white privilege. The new normal is we are stuck grossly inhibited, social distancing, masks, shut-downs, vaccinations, orders, no work no matter your age, me as a senior citizen, you our lives grind to a crashing halt, hopes and dreams on hold as our time on this earth grows shorter. Out of these ashes springs hope eternal, time spent working to earn wages disrupted, now spent writing critical essays, criticisms of the America we all want to see but burdened by the racist fascists supremacists, don't want the America of you and me but a savage brutal American autocracy. It was all supposed to be so easy, heaven on earth when all truth is revealed, yearned for by mostly all, unfortunately impossible to achieve we are bound and still in bonds by the earth. Essays derived from the mistrust, frustrations of being abused through oppression day after day of witnessing democracy under attack, powerless to stop it, wanting it to be gone immediately, constant suffering through four atrocious years. America in distress, boy, what a mess, the hate and all the rest.

Feb. 14, Americans seeking shade on a sunny day respite to aid you on your way. Now here this our country is seen the world over as a shady place, a dark, seedy, vicious, murderous nation of flailing, failing Democratic processes and institutions scrambling survival challenged by supremism, greed, corruption, power struggles as wealth privilege tears our government down. When autocracy finally wins out here to placate undesirable masses old extremes will be reintroduced, travel bans on all POC, separate but equal reinstalled, voter suppression will be vote denial for POC as they decide our fate much as the Nazis did or fascism conducting, organized executions, a catalyst for a violent end, all confrontation revolution for survival of multicultural freedom.

Yankie Doodle Dandee is really mean, America obscene, aberrated doubted, Uncle Sam outed subversion perversion maniacal dispersion aversion to harmful dangerous rhetoric what the heck this shit thick not trying to I found my rhymin' you don't need to be conflicted wicked not to worry I ain't in no hurry after you I got rhymes mines too no disrespect don't be jealous fools props to Ice Cube Snoop MC Ren Mac 10 50 Cent, alright then I strike with all my might ain't trying to step to you be like you take nothin' from you have no fear let me make this clear I'm a retired professional me my rhymes this here is my second career. The Great Society let all of us down that's all folks no more messing around us societal snakes slithering Democratic processes wither hither tither lean a nation without a backbone spineless desolate hatred weened vipers sidewinders seem a loathsome means to an end. As I strike with all my might have no fear let me make this clear I'm a retired professional me mine my rhymes this here is my second career.

The Farmer in the Dell was the text of it next-level shit ahead of its time hi ho away we go what the hell what is that smell illin' chillin' no change in that mind it's a fine line between that time vexed next you will find time press rewind as I strike with all my might have no fear let me make this clear I'm a retired professional me mine "n my rhymes see this here be my second career.

Let's pick this whack-ass bad-ass full metal crazy-ass military jacket shit apart give um somethin' to run to 'cause you know this be the nigga be the cause gonna come thru.

Feb. 16

Not because of something any one of us could have done it is today more than any single moment ever before in history since WWII our American Democracy can suffer injury harm caused by loathful indecency disdain for our progressive American way failed coup a teachable moment for Educators unpatriotic civilian sledgehammer decimating the moral arc of history in Constitutional government although not destroyed permanently blemished our paths forward so much more turbulent treacherous perilous shockingly expected. Where do we go from here honey baby lord lord lord?

Feb. 21

Book divided into chapters spelling out the stages of emotional development as government institutions prove detrimental to the people. As the actions first invoke mistrust disgust shock anger frustration resolve focus dedication solution resolution. This book can highlight a primary feature repeated in several treatise the condition of "if existence" a determination of reality judgmental in question of fact is any life in conjunction with a modern colonized world really a true physical social real-time event worthwhile in the elemental sense kindred safe compatible progressive or is it deplorable alienation mackination abomination we continue to endeavor to persevere just to survive humanity groveling in the mud and swamp.

DISGUST

Feb. 27

In a country that embraced lynchings as beneficial problem solving not atrocious murders it is important to understand these behaviors are motivated by appetite taste like going to your favorite bar where everybody knows your name cravings. Like wanting or needing your favorite food beverage or drugs racism oppression deprivation satisfy white supremacist insurrectionist cravings for pain suffering brutality violence against POC needed to reinforce their understanding of their dominance sole privilege of white power to suppress and reap rewards in seeing suffering loss agony despair and profit from it excessively. Needing to make others less fortunate suffer is handed down from barbarism and maintained by extremism no better way to describe aberrated perverts. Now perilous times ahead as racists systemically attack Democratic processes and institutions to fell topple the code of law to placate lying cover up cheating disparaging bullying criminalism transformation to autocracy to further enslave and corrupt permanently white savagery finally winning out the beginning of the end of freedom.

Feb. 28

Out of sight out of mind. There is a menace George Washington warned of partisan politics crippling our democracy and no one is paying attention anymore. If there was unlimited time to sway and argue back and forth opinion or obstinate greed time scarcity however is a factor now in every equation. This fact is more critical as pandemic threat posed over the past two years is just the beginning as super viral contagion and death worldwide is potentially imminent and may become the real fight as war becomes diminished by viral spread and resultant death tolls mandating science as the battleground but also suggests a dire possibility even with all nations working feverishly to the maximum effort with everything we know we can lose the fight although not surrendering we may not be able to stop the onslaught of death thus the planet will see the caretakers disappear and the meek flora and fauna will thrive on a planet healing itself from eons of abuse rendered by those caretakers. The complacency of both houses Congress and Senate to set the future govt. agenda to crisis now not the day-to-day bickering back and forth over rights or denial of them is petty ignorance vain seditious wastes time we may not have as our uncertainty about the future is greater. Just as Mother Nature can produce a quake, tidal wave, storm that devastates we cannot stop or control just shelter from we may not be able to shelter as all sanctuary may be compromised after all we are only human. Wake up, people of populated Planet Earth, you are endangering us all by silly partisan threats in pursuit of unchecked powers and subjugation of POC as a creeping menace on several fronts move to usurp our environmental taming time is scarce more than realized. Time waits for no man or woman continues when we are gone no longer here we may not have a choice no future no voice.

Mar.

As I sit listen to the fact COVID-19 Stimulus Relief Bill just out of the Senate passed after hours of antics more becoming of the Three Stooges not US Senators I am in realization it stimulated anger in seeing the waste of reason and time understanding our lives futures embroiled in constant war nothing to smile about. The best fighting force on the planet the US. Marines could not take the beachhead that is driven by cowardly white supremacists revealing aberrated minds perverted aspersions entrenched in chaos goals to subvert democracy in favor of white power autocracy jealousy exposed in deference of multicultural favorable outcomes. Scorched earth threats aired daily. State governments seek to deny rights daily and elect more extremists to continue the sabotage. The blessings of being on a beautiful blue planet in the Goldilocks Zone married by constant damage to our soil water atmosphere to the point where paradise is on the brink of collapse

Green House effect irreversible. The axis of power has evolved throughout history to be menace to populations carrying on the business of living. Life may not be the same if power diminishes rule of law, freedom or opportunity. If existence now living is under extreme duress soon may even become unrecognizable as vicious corruption wins out subjugation becomes the desirable norm. I confess to weariness fatigue as daily sociocultural war ravages like a fire that cannot be extinguished damaging our institutions our hearts and minds just by being born we all deserve so much better. Heed to these words of Jimmy Hendrix, "We are all bold as love."

Story of growing up harsh racism mixed with childhood innocence naivety curiosity stubbornness anger. Attacked by individuals, friends, family, kin, in-laws, cops, courts, even learning you cannot avoid this ignorance even achieving degreed status. Clamoring to get an education and remain nourished. Ego self-esteem confidence battered after years of successful assault by all the qualities of machination of alienation constant never ceasing indelible in every respect mind boggling injurious in ways still unknown.

Mar. 21

Freedom the lifeblood of our American heritage Democratic institutions sustaining law and order as a working system of modern progressive western civilization. Comes now with a cost an inescapable dilemma half of the American people want to tear it down making it more difficult to maintain status as the most powerful influential nation on the world political stage. Only part of our country supports remaining dominant the half remaining has to bout with these non-patriots while the whole country of China is in it to win it. They have no choice they are die-hard Machiavellian and have to comply or die in contrast here freedom of speech right to protest gather strike resist is in direct competition with the U.S. goals to win the fight with the Chinese as we are defeating ourselves in enduring the costs of American duality freedom versus citizen rights. If we continue this course and path then we will ultimately resign in defeat as our numbers will be unable to compete we lose dependence on our alliances will be vital to our future status as without it odds don't look good. Freedom may be the cause of our demise in contrast to government absolute control of citizenry the juggernaut that cultivated victory through eventual sole world dominance. Anyone willing to set aside differences and finally work together here yet? No, really anyone?

Having second thoughts about our traditions. People are buried typically in their best suits and dresses. I would think if you are going home for eternity yu would want comfort not appearances. I don't think God cares about attire. Old days it was your Sunday best or the only suit you had and it was forwarded viewing common decency. Starting to think I want to be buried in comfortable silk PJs.

Happy Monday. No deal yet for us po folks. Shit getting worse every day and Republicans complaining about knowing no place to get shoe shines. People dying from swallowing Clorox suggested by the Russian Nazi "n chief also buying guns to shoot Asians Chinese or not. Whites now alarmed about niggas trying to influence elections like Putin. This embracing bigotry is enough. Let's go to another dimension come back when the shit is fixed.

The freaks in Washington trying to get no liability for employers. You cannot sue if forced back to work should you get COVID. I don't mean to sound unnecessarily radical, but I think it's time for revolution of the people. A smart effort at good trouble to carry on the work of John Lewis.

Charlie Chaplin had it right: "Let us be free of hatred and racial inequality. Let us all unite." Trump floundering now like a fish out of water. Desperation showing as polls show him out of touch and losing big time.

My bro, I am compelled to speak of impending doom and no one discusses it because our senses have all been dulled. To the point "Elon Musk of Space X is deploying in space around the globe Skyline." So what you say. The *Terminator* movies highlighted Arnold from our future battling Skynet a global communications network with secret military applications. What is to stop the Skyline military applications from making a movie come true? We should be prepared for the worse we all know something is coming.

May choice of Sen. Kamala Harris be a winning candidate.

Thursday a good day to think of life after Trump leaves.

Senate in recess until Labor Day, guess they don't want to help those most in need.

Did they come up with something for unemployment? Nope. Dumb-ass Trump signed Exec. Order about 400. Completely worthless, Congress has purse power not him, I think if Pelosi gets a deal they can bring them back to vote.

Stupid-ass Trump talked about delayed election results and Nancy Pelosi becoming President. She responded no problem to have him "fumigated out" of the White House. RNC is going to be the biggest slumlord joke in history. Dehumans and racists will never live it down. Let all Republicans be satisfied with ingesting bleach. RNC this week fools on parade.

Police at it again shooting niggas in the back. Soon it will be time to identify the cop killer and bring street justice before trial. Dehumans spreading quickly.

RNC unbelievable rich white Dehumans lying out the side of their necks. They are trying to scare rich racists whatever color. Said to say some Trump support comes from rich deluded people of color. Their excuses is their fat rich asses. These people are batshit crazy.

Keys to success. Analysis of the terms protest and occupation present real options for the vital social changes needed immediately. Every day all around us are the tools to solve our living crisis. Required is the impetus to plan strategies utilizing these tools as elements of a people planned intervention to demonstrate power once and for all. Overwhelm govt. by stalemate they would have no choice but to concede to pass progressive laws. This is a modern concept of a bullet-less, bloodless revolution, it may be the only right way to survive govt abuse.

Didn't record it but Biden just made great comments about deficit in all areas Trump. I think it will be the greatest election defeat of all time, Biden will trample Trump. Trump incompetence is killing some and ruining most.

The violent disrupters purposely tainting every BLM (Black Lives Matter) event is having the effect of changing attitudes of voters. Black people already undesirable now have constant public attention. Common racist thinking is the violence is related to black people in the streets but this violence is being generated and paid for by rightwing organizations, neo Nazis, skinheads, KKK and so on. Protests vulnerable to violent disrupters whereas occupations can be far more focused on goal accomplishment and disrupters can be controlled.

When you want to cast a knowledgeable glance at the real U.S. replay documentary of lynchings and pay notice to the faces of the participants. Since then things have gotten worse but not by appearances. U.S. still lynching every way possible but now things are systemically endemic. I'm tired of being fleeced every day by this vicious U.S. bitch.

Mentally deficit Trump has openly stated he never had respect enough for citizens to provide the leadership of the presidency, instead preferring to enrich himself through his businesses in violation of the Hatch Act. Thus he has admitted to dereliction of duty making him a traitor to the U.S. enough already, gotdamnit.

What is happening? What's really going on? The COVID-19 pandemic pandemonium, raging fires destroying the land, global warming, rising sea levels, economy in ruin, unemployment massive joblessness, businesses collapsing, crazy fat rich white dehuman in the White House killing most everyone. Is God on vacation? Is this what it look like when God takes a break?

Is it really that hard to fix social problems? First, identify the enigma. Racism, Sexism, Social Injustice, Economic Injustice, 2 Systems of Criminal justice, Voter suppression, White malfeasance. Second, of all these issues point of origin central element is white power, money, hatred, dominance. Third, give all disenfranchised whites their due. Fourth, divide up the crumbs left, save them for little Tim at Christmas!

SHOCK

Food for thought. A knowledge of the potential outcomes of effective occupations demonstrates all problems can be solved. There are filthy-rich people that understand this. Why has not one of them already made the moves to set the people free? What stops them once they comprehend setting people free means fixing the problems on a more permanent social scale? What does this say about us (We the people)?

Trump in another term means we all become Russian Chinese Iranians embracing the abuse of the Palestinians while kissing Israel's ass.

When I look at William Barr, I am reminded of the prison seen in Hancock where Barr has his head stuck up Trump's butt.

You can't dismantle the great United States in just 4 years but Trump demonstrates a monstrously sadistic demented sex offender morally mentally deficit in failed leadership can sure give it a good try.

A Trump win, we become Russian Chinese Iranian Turkish Venezuelan Korean Black. I am already a second-class citizen. What patriot?

We have now witnessed our federal govt. altering CDC scientific info to downplay the impact of the virus. They have lied to the American people in a govt. documents and in the scientist names. This to make the Trump disaster look better. I have got to get a copy proof of government lies.

I only watched 3 min. of *The Apprentice* the whole time it ran. I don't find morbidly fat orange-white men with yellow hair and no brain entertaining.

Who will step up because it is time? Who will step up to replace the great soldier in this battle, Ruth Bader Ginsburg? I paid 5300 more in taxes the past 2 years than that bitch in the White House! Presidential family reminds me of a group of baboons in fancy gangster clothes.

I finally got it. Took me long enough. The elusive reason for all the Republican/Democratic racism resulting in the imprisonment and repression of hardworking people of color. They need all the systemic items of value money, power, property, fortune, to provide for these cocksuckers an unlimited supply of platinum dicks to suck. Welcome to America!

I now have proof. Any person that makes positive defensive comments about (Kenosha/Kyle) a minor that drove from two states away to walk down a street publicly brandishing an AR-15, threatening people then shouting 3 killing 2, is praising an obvious felonious senseless killer. Proof that Trump is not human but a Dehuman. A further translation is (Demon Human).

Elon Musk is preparing a Space Orbiter to take the public into space. Approximate cost of 1 million per person per flight. As much as I would love to be first in line at that cost I will wait for the elevator. (Wishful thinking)

More positive proof Trump is a Dehuman. What caring human being endowed with a soul would spread lies that kill. He is more like a Nazi than an American.

Trump and 1st lady both test positive for COVID-19. Quarantine both bitches at a local Washington dog pound. Where they can get down if needed.

Reckless behavior led to this. Kris my wife saddened by his infection illness. I am pissed he allowed his wife to be infected.

Time of COVID-19 presidential no-show to go. He was brain dead befo' infection, now he is a no-go for sho!

Why is it that the Dehuman POTUS is not even capable of being serious about suffering from a killer contagion? They have loaded him up with more steroids than normal treatment requires suggesting they are already using heroic measures to keep his stupid ass alive.

The POTUS owes the American people an apology. His ignorance of observing COVID-19 remedies not locking down the White House. He endangers us and the World. Maybe we will get an apology 10 years from now by the ousted loser. Dude POTUS just came to his office on drugs!

Yeah, he's drugged up and has doctors on hand and he's a fucking liar, bro. Now confirmed as a video back at White House shows POTUS is an orange-white madman acting like a rabies-infected dog. Seems he's out to kill us all. I want to start a petition to put Black Males & Females on the Endangered Species List.

I think scientists need to look into a little-known phenomenon called Presidential Election Victory Psychosis. Altered mental states affecting the health of the victor. I think it might explain a lot of the traumatic tragedy of the failure of this orange-white man POTUS.

If you are Black or a person of color hopefully you are happily maladjusted, socially/economically helpless, health deprived, 3 times more likely to have pre-conditions thus increased death rates, you are fearful of the pandemic, cops, white supremacists, racists, kinship, relationships, accidents, theft, murder, lynching, you are in danger when consuming or imbibing, you are trying to be inconspicuous even though invisible. What anxiety, huh?

If you are a White Male or Female exception made for orange-white men or women, shit is just fucked up.

I grew up in the era for all you rockers still out there, farewell to Eddie Van Halen, one of the finest guitar players on the planet. He accomplished greatness in his 65 yrs.

ANGER

In new Trump video he sez getting COVID-19 is a "blessing from God." Do we really need this jerk anywhere near the White House? Is this compassion for those 211,000 gone or those afflicted now? How much more can normalcy take from the heir apparent antichrist? The Trump Demon Human walks the earth.

It's a cold day in hell when you can't even count on truth from an infected POTUS, now he is willing to infect others for personal gain. POTUS not Harris is the monster Demon Human.

Keep yo fingers crossed, Steven Miller needs a ventilator and we can see him buried soon.

Trump acting like a whiny loser. Someone should slap some sense into him.

If you are White or colorless probably you are happily inheritance, socially/economically mobile, health secure, 5 times more likely to be in excellent condition thus low mortality rates, you are not fearful of the pandemic, cops, black nationalists, bigots, family, acquaintances, enigmas, crime, strangulation, you are in danger concealing contents of closet, you are trying to be the center of the known universe.

Blacks looking at the White community say, "Shit is all fucked up."

A Laker victory for the great Koby Bryant fanaticism is alive and well as mentally deficient people destroy property, openly breaking laws during a pandemic. Really!

With the Fed power play confirmation hearings for Judge Barrett, house speaker McConnell and POTUS have prescribed an enema for unwilling Americans. We have little damn choice but to reluctantly let it happen. Bend over, spread 'em.

The fact a judge can be voted and seated on the highest court without a single clear answer to Senators represents a juvenile wholly inadequate effort to place people that can ultimately destroy lives, livelihoods, lifestyles. We continue to tolerate this. Why? Don't think there is not a better way. I am at the point now where I go thru life with a fixed grimace.

Proposal of a better way to Confirmation of Judgeship. 1. Senate and Congressional closed hearings using Q & A, both verbal and written responses from candidates. Multiple cases can be vetted affording broader responses that can be witnessed by members. 2. Public hearings in which Americans can see more clearly to make the life choice decision. 3. Vote by both Houses and the Public. If I say there is a better way I have to demonstrate that possibility. See what you think.

I don't understand what is up with Pro-Lifers. Who cannot embrace the point of having to give birth, nurturing and lifetime commitment to an unwanted pregnancy is torturous?

Now quite apparent the United States Gov. is a haphazard collection of inefficient/ineffective bureaucracies achieving a mixed bag of tertiary legislation attempting to legitimize American institutions. Policies were not rigid enough to prevent power-hungry politicians from shredding legality leaving the vulnerability now witnessed. Even with a late start a fix for this would take decades of intelligent efforts, not uncommon but if it didn't work then now is greatly endangered. Sorry to say tragically it looks like the Wild Wild West will prevail the duration of our lives.

Nothing to conclude except our very own American Gov. is trying to kill us all having the audacity to implement as policy fringe crap about Herd mentality which presupposes 5 - 10 million infected greater numbers deceased even with 1/3 of total population infected it does not equate immunity. We are not ball less, or flocking sheep knowing something should be done not wanting to sacrifice personal freedom or comfort of home perhaps a patriotic duty is necessary. Who will step up?

FRUSTRATION

I am not a mindless cud-chewing bovine, not part of a breeding program, I do not move or flock as a herd and currently as a matter of fact I would punch in the face any freak that mentions Herd immunity as a potential remedy for a deadly virus cure.

I got it. I finally got it, Trump and his Trumpers should go to dairy country, take over farms by Imminent Domain and go fuck herds of heifers to hasten herd immunity!

Mooooy bueno. Hahaha

It is a failure of our values and moral institutions to have to entertain thoughts of why Trump supporters supposed to be people should want to infect me/others with the deadly contagion COVID-19. What have I done to them? Because I embrace governor's orders social distancing, stress truth over lies, fact over fiction, science over whimsy, democracy over autocracy, and prefer to avoid their narcissistic precognitive dementia orange-white infected contagious heifer humper.

Trumpers prefer a lying, cheating, fraud, financially corrupted phony, bigoted racially, sexually, socially, economically, a mentally unstable loudmouth bully that uses his hands to try to mold into reality the bullshit he's spouting, a narcissistic precognitive dementia orange-white infected contagious heifer humper. That's not my fault, it's theirs!

Trump nuts would say I'm too negatively focus on their candidate. Okay! Let me lay into Biden. A lifelong politician from Scranton, PA, that has made at times in his career mistakes in consideration of socially and racially charged legislation affecting American communities but has the impetus to evolve relegating his energy and attention to finding real solutions be they scientific, social, economic, ethical, morally seeking paths to progressively legislate effective remedies to cure, unify, heal, rebuild, repair, strengthen a nation and a world in need. 'Nuff said.

Proof here he is Mr. Russian. Warned by CIA, Military Intelligence, Chief of Staff that Giuliani would bring info from Russian spy Trump openly collaborates with Russia taking a publicity photo in the Oval Office highlighting tainted hoax crap committing treason to win. If he walks like a traitor, smells like a traitor, smiles like a traitor, acts like a traitor, Trump is a compromised American/Russian traitor.

In 16 days America is either reborn or we watch it rapidly die over the next 4 years. It is like the Big Bang all over again. The universe gave us a chance. What will we do with it?

Hope for the future. New Zealand Prime Minister Jacinda Ardern made all the right moves for by her nation they are COVID-19 free to open businesses, schools, malls, entertainment venues, a Trump victory may mandate relocation our lives might depend on it. Been honestly checking it out. Go Dodgers!

I was done when he lied to the people on his first day in office when he said, "White supremacists are good people," he cannot utter the words "Black Lives Matter," he cannot remember the names of fallen military heroes as he disrespects their wives calls them & Blue Ribbon families stupid losers, he disses and touches inappropriately intelligent women, he despises the poor will remove ACA, Roe v. Wade, destroying all conservation areas including rescinding clean air standards, no response to hurricane victims, Puerto Rico paper towels instead, no response to COVID-19 pandemic, destroyed economy using stupid tariffs, he will leave nothing but scorched remains many of them human here and throughout the world. How? Why? Would anyone sane person want this? A vote for Trump is a vote for self-annihilation. He will play golf while we all die. Not enough said.

Mitch McConnell, devil incarnate Senate Majority Leader, could not speak a normative intelligent answer to his opponent in recent debate rudely instead laughing as a devil anticipating further mayhem sinister corrupted deeds.

After all this & that. Is the real danger a potential Trump victory or is it a greater danger his followers apparently wanting to harm, scorch all decent hardworking reality-based conscientious caring persons for lack of intolerable extremism or a death wish?

Damn unfortunate! It is such a gorgeous pretty blue planet in such well-lit little corner of a spiral galaxy, a black hole at its center we have as yet to use to accomplish achieving gravity well-generated flight folding space to get acquainted with our extraterrestrial neighbors more quickly. So much to look forward to. Or is it just all for them?

The more I hear Trump utterances, the more I see some people like a fat narcissistic orange-white infantile precognitive dementia soulless lying cheating self-serving asshole. How do those characteristics make a quality Leader? Why would you make that choice? What's up with Trumpers besides systemic treachery?

Time for a heart-to-heart with Trumpers. What do they really want? A soulless nation with people of color without visibility or a voice. Lifeless cities with only white-owned businesses and white families can after attrition earn part of business and corporate profits, military of zombies racist heartless incapable of achieving or protecting, streets controlled by para-military cop murderers armed with assault weapons, citizen protests put down by brutal lethal force, laws denying rights to all poor, no government medical coverage, unchecked poverty augmented by success of the wealthy only, eventual relocation to another planet or dimension of all people of color. Once in the open healing can begin with Mint Julips for everyone.

Now he's done it. Trump has ruined my childhood years. I grew up watching *Flintstones*. I was just traumatized seeing Trump looks like a taller version of Barney Rubble. Betty was much nicer than the 1st lady. With everything around us in ruin it's no wonder after all Trump is a knuckle-dragging Neanderthal. No offense to this capable specie.

It took 5 days to get water to the Superdome, Barbara Bush said the poor stranded there without working toilets were better off. Been trying to get Trump taxes for 4 years, took them equivalent time to find Trump Chinese bank account. Currently Trump sez our biggest adversary is China, however Russia has been killing people all over the free world. Who would have a bank account supporting our foes? Trump wrongly presupposes money will shelter him from Russian mayhem or foul play. Russian Oligarchs far more rich than Trump have come up missing never seen again. A bank account anywhere in the world cannot hide over six weeks. Why 4 years? They find my banking shit right away. They would have found that account right away if it was a person of color. This two-tiered crap everything here is now whitewashed. Shit only works right here if Tom Sawyer whitewashes it all first to Becky Thatcher's approval.

Which brings me to the next unfortunate brazen "in your face" verity, "try making something out of shit and you will see what life is like for po niggas living in the USA." Living the dream, Ma, living the dream!

Now a study from Columbia University demonstrates the slow botched Fed. Non-response to the COVID-19 epidemic has cost 210,000 lives. It translates to only 13,000 dead at this moment had they done the right human response. Trump according to this study has caused a horrifying death toll and with the new rise in cases nationwide continuing mortality and new wave with flu season you feeling lucky, America? Home of the Free, in danger in every way if he has his way more death and decay ery day ery day ery day ery day ery day ery day ery day.

The final debate spells the final failing score for the final election that will finally rid us finally from the final breath and grip of the Trump regime. Finally long live freedom from Trump daily crazy.

News flash Trump uses his hands making sweeping gestures as he speaks. Hitler gestured up and down vertically saying Heil, Trump gestures right to left horizontally saying Dos Vadonna or kiss my fat orange-white Russian ass. Hitler killed over six million. Trump on course to kill more due to paper towel response to a deadly virus. As if nose blowing will provide a cure for pandemic symptoms. Also note neither Hitler nor Trump will ever say, "God bless America"!

Today U.S. set new single-day total of 83,000 cases not to mention those not detected. The graphs tracking COVID-19 cases spiking up throughout America, but just yesterday in the last presidential debate Trump said, "The numbers are going down, we are opening up in good shape, our methods were a success." Clearly Trump (Boris) is a little off with his information, maybe he's distracted by 1st lady (Natasha) picking grooming the ticks off him.

To say the least we should all be scurred trumps a big hairy beast.

One American tragedy a POTUS incapable of achieving empathy, so self-absorbed greedy hoarding every option to increase his personal gain wealth unchecked power he is willing to sacrifice neglect all Americans, letting everyone die to complete his fiendish pact with Putin. Some wealthy benefit from his abuse of the income tax system all will pay no matter your wealth because of a killer virus running rampant assisted by the vicious actions of Trump cronyism goal to infect everyone and disable the U.S. Beware the Ides of Nov. 3.

There is a domesticated creature in the animal kingdom with similar Trump fetish ass-smelling, hoarding, greedy, filthy, muddy, boorish, pink-orange-white, snorting, rooter. It's not a chicken, rhymes with bovine (plug in creature here).

I was just listening to friends talk about the load of wealthy/young black men gonna vote for Trump. This puzzles me. I have known for years every Republican administrtion redirects wealth using taxation and other means to incentivize stars, athletes, corporate execs, businesses/financial institutions while whittling away the middle class out right dismantling gentrification of poor communities in our neighborhoods. Things have not changed in this respect. Modernity has presented alternatives to the selfish I gotta get mine thinking. Lifting as we climb presupposes leaving no one behind! Does the dream entail only wealthy at the top in control? Seems a rather selfish way to think and behave reflecting on sacrifices made by my father and yours to serve this nation for some the ultimate. I cannot embrace or justify voting for Trump's pact with Putin, the goal of infecting the people disabling these U.S. for personal gain. I ask is this really because we have little faith, can't stand our neighbors, want/desire more than others, know we are especially better than the rest, you are the shit? Maximize the love humanity will reward all efforts. Minimize hate or perhaps we all die. Remember whatever wealth you contribute will buy a person of color only more time. In the final outcome when the eventual plan is to relocate people of color to another planet or dimension it will take longer but money will not save anyone, you will go also. What's to think about?

I am most uncomfortable in my choice to live in a country where at least 40 percent of populous supports a world public menace a POTUS whose vanity need to be worshipped mad grab for money more power remains purposely lofty using naivete as excuse for inexcusable failure of presidential administration to meet needs of the majority of the American people. This is a rich orange-white men's tactic to deflect blame for fatality and criminal negligence. No person of color could ever use this excuse, it is reserved from those coming from a position of power. A direct example of this atrociously apologetic yet fallibly responsible nation for as a result of human relocation caused all we live now. To personally relocate is expensive there is nowhere to run or shelter from extremism. Best of luck help those in need.

We have to find a way to place identifying marks on supremacist extremism so we can recognize what scum you are dealing with first hand. People of color are marked for life, extremists are camouflaged. This would effectively change the social equation. With treachery and deceit in the open new dynamics in psycho-social interaction may inspire change needed for centuries. When all is revealed truth and justice may triumph. Keep fingers crossed!

Boils down to wanting. What do we all want? Trying to satisfy all the desires, wishes, needs, wants, gives, for everyone. The Beatles had it right. You can't always get what you want, problem is many can't get what they need due to extremist haters need to stop you from getting it for various disturbing reasons. So much turbulence in our lives over wants and needs. We should be slow to seek selfish satisfaction pursuant of intensified live and let live. Human beings matter.

Trump in recent rally sez, "The news talks of COVID-19 too much. Everything all day long is COVID, COVID, after Nov. 4 you won't here so much about it." He sez, "In other countries people with pre-conditions that get COVID-19 are not reported so their numbers are lower." He has outright admitted in a Democratic republic he wants to sensor disable important valuable public information. He then altered info to fit his dishonest schema of why we aren't doing as well because it's a subject that haunts Trump death dying and more dying not the way he wants. COVID-19 doesn't give him the glory of a war and it is something he could have beaten without tanks and bombs so it does not meet his needs negatively exposing his inadequacy, ineptitude, incompetence, incontinence, inevitable inability to perform for the people even his wife and family. Also we will know by landslide Nov. 3. Biden camp must Beware Ides of Nov. 3. Trump cronies are poor losers, will stop at nothing, no low plateau is low as can go they know.

One disturbing note Trump and staff including chief of staff have stated they will not attempt to control the virus. "We have rounded the corner on the virus, it's going away, kids 90 o/o immune. We should open all cities, because we cannot shut down." As long as I can recall parental efforts to rid households of cold or contagion mimicked public health and safety. The measles, chicken pox, colds & flu, meningitis, polio, mononucleosis, lice, even acne. The modus operandi was first clean surroundings, appropriate warmth, medicinal support including in-person visit or house call. These days critical care nurses available by phone. To control, comfort, cure what ails you. What in the mother complaining heck is going on when the best-kept house in the world is a pandemic hot spot? You tell me!

Lakers and Dodgers have paved a path forward setting the best example for the country, nation and the World. Defending the Championship is the stride from now on. A winning spirit, a psyche motivating us to charge at the future with great determination dedicated to forging a path back to win again. Let us learn from their winning efforts to forge a new path vote vote vote to bring us all to the winning path and be rid once and for all of the lying, cheating orange-white public health national worldwide menace. Public's turn to let's play ball. Vote.

Here's what I got. Just watched a commercial paid for by Org. for Immigration Reform. Theme something like this: "Do you want to let criminals in or build a wall, Do you want undocumented on our streets or law and order, A country that gives your jobs to foreign workers?" This sinister twisting of the facts sways non-educated types and racist haters. Odd that Trump and twisted supporters spend money on tactics to deceive an American public incredibly astute at deception as a result of our slave history and more recently the Cold War. Trump and cronies spend enormous money and propaganda, they are confident they can pull the wool over the eyes of the intelligent people of this great nation they are fooling themselves. Maybe if they didn't fondle themselves so often they could do better at governing or winning an election.

Ok. What's up with the growing militia movement? Bunch of narrow-minded wealthy narcissists needing to be seen brandishing assault weapons to compensate for unfulfilled needs due to problems with bed wetting, failure to launch, excessive insecurities concealing contents of closet, outright cowards. Easier to stand with a group of fellow weirdos than to work for real solutions. They are utter waste of time.

We are in a bad way. 80,000 new cases reported Europe imposing new lockdown methods. New contagion and deaths on the rise. With the current rate of infection including hospitalization soon overcrowding will threaten intensive care options. We may have to regulate days when citizens can shop for supplies and each trip now becomes more dangerous. We as a family are following scientific social guidelines but with so many that take safety for granted we must be rigorously protectively cautious. In 5 days we can start down a road with intelligent clear solutions if all goes well. Election this time is a clear choice. Life over death. Let us all vote to stay alive.

RESOLVE

Seems to me. If the stuff be broke sometimes you got to fix things first before you can make plans. The economy is broke reflected daily by actions in the stock market, entertainment and social venues shut down mostly more to follow, colleges, universities down, bars, local and national parks, things are getting crucial, really hard to get a good martini. What sane administration would not make the effort to fix things first especially when it means saving lives before seeking personal gratification for satisfying racist supremacist greedy obscene fetish desires of a wannabe dictator with harem?

Bad time now to make a poor life choice. I say this especially and specifically framed to express contrast. With things the way they are national worldwide scenarios crucially combating what starts to look like the pre-verbal biblical end of days everyone choose wisely. I'm reminded of a line in a modern movie, "he chose poorly." Imagine outcomes here, please, y'all.

I see Trump gets high on the power of being in front of the mike & audience or unruly crowd at his rallies, you judge. Super-spreader events led by Mr. COVID-19 American Russian traitor seeking out new ways to infect us but get higher and higher himself a user abuser misuser loser addicted to harming most for the pleasure of the few. Trump has multiple addictions, refuses help. Wish we could have known. Would've saved a lot of grief, pain, suffering, disaster, deaths.

I forget to add false sense of being a deity. Trump enigma will leave us all with unwanted but unavoidable PTSD? Seek professional cures.

I'm puzzled how Trump stands in front of thinking people each understands the virus has reached new high in infection levels and he deceives saying, "It's rounding the corner, it's rounding the corner." It is a verbally stated delusion to minimalize and redirect the pain and suffering outweigh the gains for most.

Trump in rally asks, "What if I lose the election? What will I do if I lose?" Curious Trump being the sole shot caller, "Proud boys, stand up, stand back," he needs no help with anything running ruining our nation socially, economically, medically. So is/was the obese infectious contagious contaminated apocalyptic morose Dehuman trying to be cute, shy, coy, or just hard to swallow?

Something his hideous don't escape frightening. If he really wants a vision post-election defeat I suggest he leave the great US give up passport citizenship, take up permanent residence in Mother Russia. My homies, are you wit me?

Just heard a Trump supporter, a white female at a Michigan rally, say, "The nation is not in a good spot right now, I believe Trump can move us forward." Trump wants to censor valuable public information, suppress eliminate voter rights, taint valuable scientific public health emergency procedures, destroy preexisting condition treatment options, legislate away ACA, Roe v. Wade, gerrymander all districts, remove Voter Rights Act, taxation obliteration of the middle class, no federal response to any national crisis neglecting all human casualties as acceptable, continuation of self-enrichment in direct chronic violation of emoluments clause, violation in use of the people's house, destruction of our foreign policy contributing to worldwide embarrassment, neglecting our troops' allies, commitments, treaties, society, citizens, environment, no response to global warming threat, pandemic, national security endangered. She evidently is a modern white female conservative psychotic digesting the Trump regurgitations verbally flatulating the undigested fodder of essential lies accompanied by sinister demeaning comments to excite them feeding deranged hollow empty compliments they embrace for dear life as if they bring redemption from the antichrist corrupted deluded rapped of the limited sense they momma gave them disciples of death the Trump regime enigma. Lord, help us, the flock is blinded. Does not see.

After 4 years of sustained assault by incumbents I guess we should feel pride in the notable strength of our sociopolitical economic institutional systems able to withstand such critical targeted attacks designed by traitorous self-seeking cowards for power and money. They have given us all up so current first family disgracefully helps itself stealing from destroying the national cookie jar. Greedy obsessively wanting all for yourself is nothing new most adults secure in conduct have learned beyond this vice. I am certain now immaturity is a part of the psychiatric disaster that is Trump. I played king of the hill as a child growing up understanding the win is to defeat another. Tempering victory became critical to maintaining friendships and limiting injury. Incumbents are unconcerned with the health and welfare of the presumed majority of Americans. Ebeneezer Scrooge would learn from Trump ways of the salamander seeking finding more scum. When you have bottomed out you can go no lower. Trump is bottomed out, we can do so much better. Rise up, take back the nation. Progressive Democratic freedom from Trump abuse we take back the hill.

Sorry I missed this. Trump supporters are most grievously suffering, they are critically crucially needing cures for asymptomatic psychiatrically fettered mentally developmental psychosis cancerous in its spread and obliteration of infected regions of the brain. Needless to say most are brain dead. Suggesting humanitarian ethic they be put down a painless effective remedy.

Tomorrow's election 1 mo 2 go for what you know. Either Let's Go or Psycho!

Biden will have millions more votes than Trump. The nightmare is the callous cruelty of early constitutional legislators wove into the spine of freedom the Electoral College, I've heard it called "slavery's revenge on the 21st century," it is hold card of the institution of white control over the masses denying the people "popular vote." It was done in consideration of the white accusations the "people are too frivolous to make intelligent voting choices." It is a genuinely paranoid conservative white mechanism to manipulate power maintaining control due to antiquated fears. The Electoral College stands in the way of Freedom. Fingers crossed Blue moves us forward.

Solar Power Molten Core Mass Thermal Electromagnetic Field Energy Exchange Dynamics. Remind me this is the way to fly. The best spaceship should be similar in design to the most successful spaceship under our feet. Why would think tank egg heads imagine, draw, craft as rockets, or saucers, more or less flying bombs? Why not a craft more like that good ole example earth? Although anti-matter exists like the 4-million-year-old dinosaur shit whites used contaminating us and the World, there's no reason to get anywhere near that. Know where anti-matter is and adequately protect yourself and others from it. Why go to Mars in a spaceship powered by a needy high-maintenance dirty bomb capable of obliterating the known Universe? A Solar Energy Spaceship using a Molten Core Mass to generate Thermal Electromagnetic Field Energy Exchange Dynamics can create the unlimited heat, speed, and field energy to accomplish charged particle flight. Sub-light speed but can put you on the Moon or Mars in a few minutes maybe even hours, not years? A bottle of Spirits the Crab Nebula, Crackers, Brie easily.

On an election day in 2020 clearly results demonstrate how apparently brutally ugly our country has become when an impeached rogue greedy lying traitor has a chance for a second term. The Electoral College machination specter of death on Democracy looms as anarchy, racism, supremism, voter suppression, cultism, dismantling of fair judicial practices, economic rape of American resources, moral ethical departure from traditional norms favoring psychotic chaotic, corruption of law enforcement to embrace white mass murderers and felons tiered to leniency, corruption of courts at all levels, legislative impudence crippling any economic social relief to the poor, continuing demolition of the middle class, attack on the black community, separate attacks on Latino communities, denigration continuing attacks on women to destroy Obamacare, Roe v. Wade, gerrymander all districts, renewed efforts at the criminal inhuman practice of separation of children at the border, abandonment of all pacts, treaties, allies virtually dissolving primary defensive relations, neglect of international foreign trade and policies, no responses to life-threatening issues administration neglect of all U.S. preferring civilian deaths to rational clinically sane scientific solutions. Wild Wild West my ass, this is full-blown 3rd-world failure of historical commitments of the U.S. to protect freedom Democratic values and patriots many making the ultimate sacrifice determined to position is freedom bound only to fail due to the frailty of a political system to prevent intelligence spoilage through degradation of social bonds creating an ethical corrupting contaminate denying all fairness permanently to all men and women.

I am beyond horrified and shocked at the new American psycho crazy image displayed by wealthy empowered racist fascist supremists dissidents many Senators and Congressional Representatives embracing the goal of fascist dictatorship crippling this Democratic republic. In the war patriots fought died for everyone anarchists, racists, self-serving arrogant demigods, revolutionaries, dissidents, by winning wars against freedom on other shores we forgot to dig in here stateside. We got complacent too comfortable thinking this experiment is working well, I assure you for hardworking, normative, patriotic duty-bound whistle blowers, intelligent, conscientious, taxpayers, dedicated to the freedom promise our system should now be on the endangered list of toppled governments possibly never to recover. Too bad after all we have worked for the final outcome may be we all kill each other trying to fight to stay alive. Unwilling we must resign ourselves to the outcomes of the great tragedy America burning down.

If this change in American values means I should teach in my home intolerance, hate, bigotry, racism, violent extremism, contempt, arrogance haughtiness, disregard for human suffering, greed, jealousy, psychotic desires, fetishes, abnormal behaviors reinforcing civic unrest, encourage vice, corruption, malign impugn presumed American values and communities. I resolve my household will not be desecrated by uncontrollable failures to maintain a civil respectful common decency in our collapsing disappearing America. Looks like a change now inevitable. Out with the old, dead and stankin'. In with a squinting scant view of hope. Thank the wholly Universe.

Diminished path to win Trump claims victory continuing the buffoonery common to someone paranoid psychotic chaotic trash talk coming out the side of his neck. Delusional now knows debt and court trials into taxes and other abuses of power will put him and family behind bars including economic criminal penalties. So be it.

We may mercifully still have a slim chance to try to heal America and the World. Global warming is just or more a danger than the pandemic now murdering our kind everywhere on Earth. When faced with impossible odds throughout human history we have overcome risen above mankind has triumphed. Now faced with worldwide life-threatening enigma the crunch pressure to fix resolve find solutions is on. If done right Mankind has the remote chance possibility of making a giant leap forward in scientific remedy technology as multiple threats demand we prove ourselves to continue as viable not doomed. We must all step up now.

News reporting of vote counts suggest having some miniscule renewed faith in the American voter not to be fooled by sinister cowardly false leadership preferring a better path to organized universally shared accepted values of sociopolitical economic developmental Freedom. Time to work together to make us greater together. Thank the stars life love without Trump.

Biden will win. Now we must turn the tide of racism charging towards us like Bison. We need a nationwide social exchange program televised reality TV *House to House*. Men and Women temporarily taking up residence in racially diverse different homes sampling problems then work on visible solutions amenable to most everyone. We need a new way to shape a new day.

Now we come to reckon with the mundane inexorably unavoidable fact institutional racism supremism is a guiding motivator in our national sociopolitical economic developmental framework we all need a time-out, reprimand, tempering, honing, chiseling if necessary mandated introspective social discussions, criticism, role play, psycho drama, interactive meditated active robust cutting-edge intrusive, targeting society tolerance intolerance maintenance social psychological repair of our national intellectual framework. I suggest a new reality show: *House to House*. Premise for occupants to trade places in each home. Living facing day to day. Ground rules avoid violent confrontations. Challenges to face social issues head on. Match sessions 1st. Shouting all conduct filmed not censored. 2nd. Verbal expressed criticisms. All are accepted. 3rd. Professional Responsible Resourceful Intervention. 4th. Potential Resolutions 5th. Agreement 6th. Shocking Unexpected. Previews of next episode. Title of premier show "My New Neighbors Are Niggers." I think it would do better than *Naked and Afraid*.

Election called Biden 46ᵗʰ President of these United States.
Today's energy is visibly notably hyper positive good for the drama of Election 2020, public actions motioning us toward the rampaging pandemic ravaging killing millions in its wake. Global warming bringing catastrophic changes to populations 'round the world carving

new fault of human settlements throughout our planetary home. Earth besides natural disastrous culling events charging us down like a herd of buffalo, close election results point to disturbing outcomes a criminal psychotic chaotic impeached rogue got the second most popular votes in history correspondingly fifty percent of taxpaying citizens some could be your neighbor, coworkers, employee, associate, business partner, mistress, tailor, waiter, bartender, doctor, lawyer, electrician, pilot, pharmacist, banker, barber, stylist, star, athletes, the factors motivating voters to choose death over life need to be closely examined as a clear answer picture must be drawn up to produce a Social Analysis into making choices preferring psychotic chaotic answers to psycho sociopolitical factors influencing all American lives, the other fifty percent embracing life preferences to manage the buffalo stampede unifying reason and desire to render national intelligent framework growth in tolerance as normalcy intolerance as identifiably detrimental extreme undesirable. A psychological profile of character traits linking private choices to selections favoring psychotic chaotic mayhem.

Vice President elect Kamala Harris, I heard first tonight, Oh, What a Relief to see hear discern truth commitment compassion disciplined professionalism in her presentation of winning the most important election of our time. President-Elect Joe Biden actually jogged to the podium about 10 yards, Trump couldn't jog 2, the Biden speech did not disappoint addressing everyone in our nation and the world, he they will deliver remedies of hope improved opportunities working sociopolitical mechanisms guiding us down Freedom's path to a more civil conscientious non-hater glorified greater America.

Solar Power Molten Core Mass Thermal Electromagnetic Field Energy Exchange Dynamics uses charged field energy created by dynamic molten core field energy interactions with Electromagnetic Field Energy forces surrounding the craft thanks to either light or dark matter energy. In motion it would appear as a white intensely bright glowing spark charging or discharging enabling intense propulsion speed transversing navigations to compel super-hyper-accelerated spaceflight.

Footnote. Craft might become invisible to the observer in flight.

Don't think you have to achieve light speed to travel vast distances in space or time travel just fast as the space itself, you become a part of it as it recoils post-initial bending of space time when targeting your destination using a reaction generated by ununpentium modulation dynamic disruption harmonic field density frequency alignment stabilizer. Let space do the hard work.

IE. Controlled Gravity well.

Mind blower the cost of rocket fuel inhibits has slowed progress in space-oriented programs which still involve continued usage of 4-million-year-old dinosaur poop gobbling up international budgets with no remorse for contamination climate impact sustainability solar craft enjoy limitless clean field energy fuel absolutely free in conjunction with a core mass constantly generating active field energy as well molten iron or nickel cores are inexpensive with little to no fuel cost expenses, capital can be directed to other primary high-demand requirements microchip processors including nano technology.

Trump has not yet conceded. Kushner approached the uncontrollable wailing baby to suggest he do so. Truth is the brainless broke fraud has another chance if he could muster the adult demonstrate professional dignity mobilizing Republican misfits to run again in 4 yrs. Sadly 2024 may repeat Election agony 2020. Let's hope not. Power to the people.

A good friend told me talk to Elon Musk waste of time, here's why.

Problem like that they are full of themselves will let first their pride then arrogance in their highly commendable reusable smart rockets fashionably late antiquated due to socioeconomic sluggishness, they should have been here by the eighties at the outside hard to get conceited to acknowledge they are ass backwards.

Biden/Harris just two days after Election acceptance speech naming COVID-19 Emergency Task Force announced will reverse Trump foreign policy blunders, rejoin valuable alliances ready to display the right correct energy remedies reweaving the surgically sensible social sinews stimulating synaptic social sutures reconstructing psychosocial societal fabric framework. Refreshing to behold once again finally sensible responsible patterns of governing.

There is an added advantage to navigating space on the Solar Power Molten Core Mass Thermal Electromagnetic Field Energy Exchange Dynamics spaceship I described the constant intense heat/thermal exchanges can easily generate more than adequate pressure conditions to incubate diamonds during flights, a byproduct of ship design features.

Each flight of the spaceship can produce over 1000 times the initial cost including concepts of organized scheduled flights to build enrich the national economy to the point where for the first time in over 100 years real property can be realized and produce better quality of life eventually shared worldwide wealth because for the first time in our lives wealth will be finally willingly more generously widespread escaping scarcity definitions opening new doors to human progressive futures.

Prosperity is something the losing administration said was coming is not possible here in the U.S. Our system creates conditions that maintain impoverished lifestyles for the majority granting wealth and opportunity to the lucky through inheritance, educational financial prowess, natural physical ability, good fortune, lottery affecting a small minority. We do not share wealth because we view it as scarce, mostly inaccessible out of reach.

In the new thinking era of modernity we can embrace concepts of wealth without jealousy and Real Politik misconceptions we can depart from aberrated misconceptions emerging as the Phoenix in a *Harry Potter* movie renewal of the shape of our ideas allowing freedoms visualized but never witnessed as positive futuristic human outcomes.

Please join me in the knowledge of expectation, our lives do not have to be bound by obstacles, poverty, hopelessness, inopportunity, despair, helplessness, hate, jealousy, out-of-reach seemingly impossible goals even desires when we shed the purposeful bonds of psychosocial restraint unlock our deserved awarenesses to know a path exists to a better life and future of wealth and prosperty universally shared.

It is apparent incredible it is oscillating with expansion resilience all around us our nation jump starting transitioning low gears to kick into high speed having been stalled by intentional willing vicious political sabotage using incompetence as alibi for criminal traitorous conduct causing enormous death suffering further economic institutional destructive dissolution of societal norms erodes our dependency relationship with government protections disregard for our vulnerability is beyond contemptable and human compassion. Americans deserve have earned are entitled to the promise blessings so many have fought, endured, died for. Fantastic new opportunities await as we shed the unwanted baggage of uncertainty moving instead to brave bold new promise of a freedom that looms close beckoning welcome.

According to Mary Trump, "My Uncle Will Break as Much as He Can," nothing unpredictable, "I say when a bull gets in a China shop you expect to replace everything." Why did we put a bull in a China shop anyway, please tell me?

Finally a reduction of white male orange-white vanity and testosterone in the Executive Branch of the American Government, let's hope it's not too little too late to begin maintenance repairs of the 700 years of man's inhumanity to man crippling human social progress violence hatred killing has poisoned our past present continuing moving parallel with passing generations competing with intelligence reason to destroy future as well vigilance is required a steadfast adherence to protecting the essence the contributions of Women's Work tempering the Wild Wild West making it safe again for us all "Lifting as We Climb."

Let me ask you a question. Is there ever a situation when generously safely offered no strings attached Everyone's Universal Concept of Paradise would you refuse it? If so, Why? Answering this question you assume Paradise is tangible or real. A fiction or prediction Paradise is actually a concept of life more completely satisfying all dreams desires. Paradise seems potentially possible in the future of human experience because we are in a position to recover ancient values lost over time corrupted by greed population historical expansionism. We can retrieve the lost values of Mohenjo-Daro paradise lost.

As a nation we mourn our dead while white male orange-white Russian traitorous loser slips into manic delusional asymptomatic multiple psychosis confused as power recedes continuing the practice of taking up space not enabling the office of ODNI to officially work at transition transfer of authority, same old same old as Barr defaces his own career as a failure POTUS Ass Kisser, slowing impeding forward moves which need to go being we have already lost so much time. Even though the people have spoken we still have to watch the white man loser now with a new slant sympathetic news coverage distasteful palatable only because we are assured Trump "will have no more good days in his fat white greedy life" post the greatest Election loss of all time. Good Riddance.

Apparently after years of watching NASA launches each one costing multi-millions of dollars in fuel and engineering technology costs we knew after all the years spaceflight is enormously expensive using their ideas. Seems like another brainwashing we were unaware convincing us there way is theoretically sound practical worthwhile when in fact it has served to throw our nation into economic sluggishness only capable of progress at their ridiculous pace. When you wake up from the cultivated false respect realizing their accomplishments have been few but celebrated disgust leads to the truth. A different spaceflight vehicle can use safe fuel at little to no cost instead of costing multi-millions each flight a new design can also create wealth with each flight consider now space exploration so easily affordable every flight can increase our nationalists' wealth stockpiles. What are we waiting for, Jesus to come and point the way?

I guess we really can't blame privileged wealthy white's scholars, graduates with status rank limitless opportunity beyond norms perks offered to those occupying positions of governmental reverence for failure to negotiate the pitfall stuck on stupid.

Now the "coup de grace" this nation is a trap primarily as law perceived in Constitutional terms with the exception of legislatively imposed taxation presumably legitimate disfigured by political greed corruption to the point of national blinding tactics used to distort public perceptions of day-to-day press, publicity web colleges universities think tanks radio broadcasts culpable for asymptomatic unearned pride patriotism exactly what their deceptions are targeted to achieve complacency neglect "I don't care" attitudes. How else can you explain the disaster of a Trump presidency? It was predetermined. Knowing where we live shouldn't be a surprise to anyone.

Now we know the magic behind the great NASA illusion trick, keep in mind they are still using the beaten like a dead horse same old scientific unsustainably gouging horrendously costly high school basic Rocketry methods. Why? To continue to extort money from taxpayers using the space program budget as excuse to slow walk program goals and gains continuing to deceive taxpayers for military defense spending or other dark water projects publicly funded used for dark ulterior motives, it is a matter of time until more and more taxpayers realize this government-sponsored deception.

Here's one of you all imagine, a government-sponsored program never before conceived in any human history or imagination construct: Government Distribution of Wealth to Taxpayers, normalized regular distribution schedules throughout all the states representing our nation not Socialism but reward for willing civilian participation in the most profitable successful Space Program ever conceived or imagined or constructed. How 'bout dat? Could you hang? Si o No? Que Bien?

Ok. I have a few minutes between workout and dinner prep, I'm dying to tell you where the Diamonds are made in the craft, ok ok in the chamber housing the Molten Core Mass contained in interactive specifically modified modules the core mass forms a mantle of carbon silicates which are under continuing consistent thermal pressure energy compressed into the tops of the core reaction modules where they can be monitored by core maintenance they are almost shock absorbers between core modules and ship's inner hull the mantle reaction takes only minute, core material leaving 99.67778-percent material for energy uses. You can be able to visually see them at different stages of process, I speculate production of appropriately 10,000 diamonds per square foot looking at a reaction chamber of about 5000 feet in circumference. Perfect diamonds, you do the math.

A friend suggests having diamonds in such abundant quantities would make them less rare, I suggest finding more oil, did not diminish rarity they would be regulated by socioeconomic Macro Micro market economy management relevant to international exchange rates in market shares values unique to multicultural international market economies. Sorry, been a long time since Econ 101. But, I think more diamonds in the world translates to more for everyone.

Now enlightened there is a different way to get to space safer less costly to conduct active energetic programs greater employment new goals that are achievable not out of reach casting aside the antiquated cost-gouging horrendously disabling fuel necessities for a cleaner nonpolluting craft design and energy sources compatible with sane intentions not to be inconsiderate polluters of our universe but amiable conscientious caring explorers safely using space shared by all instead of now threatening to take dirty antimatter reactors to Mars which is not avoidance of stuck on stupid but is a good way to contaminate all space. Now visible even with perfect options for a better way powers that be for ulterior motives are continuing the course to be the slowest most dangerous callous incompetent polluters using inferior costly dangerous designs to maintain the death grip relationship with the Oil and Gas industries. This vicious bond including contracts with electronics & communications firms continues reducing our efforts to a snail's pace. Every indication is these programs are led by similar scum to the salamander that refuses to vacate the People's house. As long as programs are run by pampered scholarly vain highly conceited self-serving arrogant demigods each asshole greased by another we will continue to live in the dark inhibited by our inability to take even a baby step beyond planned design and propulsion ineptitude failure to an obviously better way.

Ok, time to be blunt. Our endangerment begins in a region far far away in time not so long ago when desperate white men were building their farms, fences and cities having overcome the roughshod of the Wild Wild West planting crops dependent on sunlight warmed on the trail to harmless chemical combustion. Fire, dried ourselves, clothing our fields, foodstuffs supplied a consistent dependable necessary warmth creating a fine lifeline all over the world. What was the reason during the start of the industrial revolution man looked down started digging up 4-million-year-old dinosaur poop as deep and hard as it is to get the offensive horrible odor the mess of geysers contaminating poisoning right from the start then to actually put their hands in it. Really? Really? Why dig into the dirt and filth when solar power is visible no digging clean no mess odor not poisonous non-contaminating easier to access control manage superior as tool for every need yet we continue to be poisoned daily as a result of now apparently efforts related to selfish maniacal endeavors over extreme greedy acquisition of wealth power economic control now guilty of casting aside whole generations of working class currently still as unconcerned about the current generation being used abused misused taken advantage of cheated harmed maligned by same old incessant criminal abuse of planned obsolescence.

Crunch is on 144,000, new cases breaking records higher infection rates daily across the country. Crisis detected this is a life-threatening major emergency if you dig way deep into subterranean scum turn over a rock you will find the frantic pouting obese loser, "The Weeping Salamander" in charge of mechanisms that can save American lives instead preferring future planning on self-indulgence not stopping a deadly contagion treating the horror of American deaths as tolerable acceptable. I have grown so tired of seeing Trump's mug, I now only see him as "The Weeping Salamander." A salamander wallows in death and decay no wonder we are cure stagnant we have to move on the National threat that is "The Weeping Salamander" and then we can move like the robots seen in Pacific Rim to battle defeat COVID-19 then we can take domestic terrorist militia.

Ladies and gentlemen, let me introduce you to our future quite unexpected. A scientific breakthrough paving the way for more fantastic journey into the future of human potential. We are awaiting the birth and development of for lack of a better whole description "Smart Gel," a chemical compound worked on in a lab that by amazing divine coincidence of a lab accident working with embryonic growth compounds microchip processor design enhancements interrelated with Nano technology the accident produced sentience in the gel compound creating a new lifeform. Resulting in a Smart Gel after communication with it raised awarenesses, the gel is dedicated to protecting mankind from harm because it recognizes we gave it life. More to follow.

Here's one for you take a walk on the ocean floor bottom of Mariana Trench or brave the intense pressure of a gas giant Jupiter for a jog. Using a Smart Gel bodysuit bearably skintight without independent oxygen supply Gel would morph at molecular level and produce unlimited oxygenation comfortably not even detecting an iota of lethal pressure extremes. I think that just put the memory of Tom Swift to shame rest in peace.

How valuable Smart Gel will become an insulator as example you could stand next to a lava cauldron protected by 1 sheet of Smart Gel only 1/8 of one inch in thickness cauldron temp 2500 degrees other side of sheet protector room temp to touch! Human in space because of catastrophic event decompressing compartment jump into Smart Gel survival assured without pressure suit accompaniment in space or aqua environment! Smart Gel will act as a catalyst hyper enhancing solar thermal energy exchange dynamics throughout ship planform design contributing to safe Charged Particle Flights.

As the nation breaks new COVID-19 records daily 159,000 yestidy,

144,000 the day before, 170,000 expected today alarming this threat we are not doing enough to stop the other vile despicable hate displayed by arrogant disenfranchised believers in a destined chosen preferred dominant race to be genetically superior. These disasters are part of over 70,000,000 people of all races colors afflicted motivated by chronic adherence to psychotic chaotic asymptomatic psychiatrically fettered mental delusions of grandeur not isolated for these obvious illness but exist side by side with hardworking wholesome healthy taxpaying citizens most commonly to help each other improving our lives. Two bulk segments of the country colliding like a strike slip fault earthquake of the Continental plate which produces great damage resulting in nothing but losses. None of this human savagery is wanted or normal. It is a byproduct of the human condition our parents are responsible for passed on to each generation a sick fault in our frail socialization infecting half of our nation and the World. Just as it is hard to get conceited to acknowledge they are stuck on stupid these malcontent socially disenfranchised believe that they are entitled by their birth into the historically criminally perceived dominant race the delusions based in past conquest victory. We have similar urgency to battle this as its rate of destruction exceeds the current pandemic. We all have work to do. Let's get at it. Bring it on, this we can get done.

Let me put this another way: If you think you should have easy access to everything we all have to work hard for, it's ok to lie all the time, cheating on taxes makes you smart, scheming on business deals is cool, robbing the innocent blind, taking advantage of women and children especially little girls is something we all do, extorting the public, destruction of democracy for profit, a sucker is born every minute, taking candy from a baby, it's ok to kill those people, chaos is a good lifestyle, treachery is honest, contempt is normal, bigotry is entitlement birthright, the south will live again, they shoot horses, don't they? lynching will solve American problems, whites only, send "em back awhare they came from, what they don't know won't hurt them, only we have that those rights, us first then them if you insist, those animals or better off, let them eat cake, always us never them, pay it no never mind, they ain't kin. There's tons more. If you answered yes or agree with any of those aberrated misconceptions you are sick borderline paranoid psychopath, seek help immediately before harm to yourself and others.

I don't know, guys, the public BS that made news as if it mattered, "Trump supporters held a post-election defeat rally in DC." for the pink pouting punk pilferer pliny phony paranoid psychopathic paraplegic pummeled primate pussy needing hugs consoling white enhanced enriched encouragement brooding reinforcement of "I am white, always right rightfully by birthright," I don't remember such rallies for losing candidates previously, now the apocastrophy deleterious spiraling decline in the structural maintenance of wholesome American values and morals vomiting Q-Anon. Those of us who know Q of *Star Trek* series know comprehend the characteristics would be Mankind's greatest threat ever truly a misfortune of galactic equivalence. Similar to Earth being threatened by Superman's foe Mizilplivk from another dimension or Avengers Wanda the Scarlett Witch, nothing but dangerous more than jailbait! We are talking about senseless cult satiation mutilation of intelligent sentience leaving behind brutally mentally misguided disfigured thought processes barely recognizably human. Much like living with creatures you can't communicate with, example *The Walking Dead*. We really can't continue to accept this lowering of the bar.

I see big trouble in Little America. Trump is in a rage. Against the machine, openly encouraging his minority of mentally disfigured crazies to organize in revolt to overthrow Election Results and take permanent control of the presidency. This is felonious criminal traitorous conspiracy to take control through violent revolution anyone else would have been arrested and charged. Trump has not read history you see for this to work he actually himself would have to lead the armed assaults wielding weapons against military trained killers, of course everyone knows he is a coward. So we can really stop this stupid crap right away if the news agencies would condemn calling out these morose juvenile tantrums then changing the diaper he has been soiling since Election night. Like any baby that has gone Trump is elated relieved confused distracted somebody in the White House, please take responsibility for the American people and Change His Damn Diaper. Please?

Ok, ok, something pleasant fantastic deserved dreamed of wildest considerations of human perceived stupendous wonderfully rare exotic profound ultimate marvelous magnificent beyond so with Smart Gel bodysuit you can get started here but go to any planet anywhere and do it different Human Beings Walking on Playing in on a Lava Lake unconcerned absolutely free of danger to self or others. The properties engineered into Smart Gel eliminate all dangers including debris impact as the bodysuit can deflect all potentially dangerous harmful materials. Ever wanted to dance on a lava flow? Probably not but would you if you could? Our good future is on the way just a few more hurdles to clear. Looking forward to a great day, a better way.

I'm thinking of the research and stress developmental specs tests necessary to run to guarantee beyond 100 0/0 flawless suit efficiency and functions. Tests on pressure variants collision impact measurements directional repulsion of debris redistribution pounds per square inch of impact repulsion heat thermal resistance tolerances internal suit temperature maintenance. Some tests might include armored truck collisions, tank impact, speedy projectile or bullet missile, flamethrowers, CO2 resistance, charging Bull Elephant Rhino, Bison. Low altitude drops insuring no protective failure.

The Great Depression and the Stock Market crash Black Friday 1929 closed banks, businesses followed economy shut-down, fortunes lost homeless encampments bread lines soup kitchens riding the rails suicides psycho somatic mental illnesses depression depravity helplessness despair scarcity never seen this pandemic is alarming close in similarly it is also apparent we did not heed valuable lessons then as we are struggling as the dominant Intelligence on this planet to eliminate suffering as we labor to demonstrate we are meeting the challenges head on battling two pandemics forward progress painfully slow due to corrupted paths silly misguided disfigured actions by the most irresponsible administration ever. When human casualties that could have been prevented are perceived as acceptable this maniacal behavior should be exposed dealt with as criminal conduct. The extremism in the two party historical tug-o-war is murderous incendiary intolerable in passing legislation to improve our lives and our nation instead preferring to stall important legislation that could positivity benefit the majority. At a time when both administrations should be using life-saving measures people's lives are inconsequential of no concern. Enough is enough. Constitutional document reads you have a right to change the government with threat pandemic levels increasing daily, we need this change sooner than later. See now everyone how incomplete frail our government worked on for 400 years is still haphazard inefficient ineffective bureaucracies. Fix this now, we are running out of time.

It has taken me too long in this blatant realization we are witness to a byproduct of white privilege silver spoon precariously unending wealth best of everything world at your feet power of extremes inheritance undigested recalcitrance phobia behavioral impudence impugning early childhood learning developmental framework for social growth instead radical learning cognitive disorder a condition untreated in this failure of family unit encouraged cultivated to become the undesired indelible anathema in real time. We had a rotten childlike mental case in the People's house. We need his procreations to take the pampered senile old phony fake remind him he has little more than 34 days to make an even bigger angry birds childish loser tantrum eruption paroxysm spectacle of his dumb ass.

Current apocastrophies machinations Trump presidency, stumbling administration transition, half of American population mentally misguided brutally disfigured barely recognizably human, extorting taxpayers, voter suppression, cultism, murderous nationwide policing, political intolerance, sinister gerrymandering, redistribution of wealth using criminal taxation, destruction of the middle class, legislative enslavement of working class, abuse of all people of color attacks on women children, attacks on immigrants. It seems if one person starts stupid shit others join in odd. When did it become posh apropos to jump headfirst into shit? Are we so weak we lend ourselves to being influenced by blind leading the blind? When is it fashionable to leap off cliff when this event promoter lies about the bottom impact being fatal? We are facing never-ending battles, our stress litmus tests are very high challenging extreme tolerances. We are growing as a culture but are we growing in the most appropriate and necessary areas to make the apocastrophies go away for good?

Now I'm gonna hab me sum fun in the Solar Power Molten Core Mass Thermal Electromagnetic Field Energy Exchange Dynamics spaceship the Living Environment is a self-contained Trans Bio Molecular Sonic Phase Dimensional Variant Habitat impenetrable impervious undetectable incredibly shielded using Trans Variant Alloys Carbonic Silicates. It is housed internally in the chamber holding the Molten Core Mass surrounded by a Smart Gel Retention Gyrating Omnispherical Bubble. Engineering, Sick Bay, Crew Quarters, Mess, Real Water space shower made possible by Molten Core Condensation, Recreation Facilities, Storage, Stellar Astro Cartography, Turbo lifts, Communications, Weapons, Holodecks. The real fun is to be living the dream to be making this dream no longer a dream but tangible verisimilar.

Daily seeing Trump anathema wantonly dismantling American institutions gutting vital systems as a surgeon without knowledge of how to use the surgical knife or the composition of what they are operationally mutilating. Official notices by the AMA, Labor Leaders, CEOs, Resignation from the Justice Dept. to not carry out chaotic carnage exposing gov. entrails, distorted troop irrational movements inviting confrontations in Iraq and Afghanistan, complete avoidance of COVID-19 joint emergency efforts, no effort by Trump regime to prevent American casualties to this pandemic in fact insuring more to die. Was this the Russian plot from the git-go? Trump, a Russian traitor, should allow contagion to run rampant weakening so many it makes entire nation vulnerable and open to attack. During the Bubonic Plague people awoke daily to dark skies the smell of burning flesh in mass graves. Waking daily here you see immediately death tolls climbing, refrigeration units brought in to store corpses unable to keep up with increasing numbers of deceased. Two pandemic slap in the face every day waky waky. What next? Trump subnormal effort to head off Covid-19 spread prepares to use nuclear weapons to strategically bomb U.S. neighborhoods to slow contagion progress. Say what? We are still in danger from a delusional asymptomatic mentally disturbed narcissistic murderer unable to cope with white man failure including others with similar proclivity for monomaniacal actions.

Next fathom to negotiate. Is our governmental day-to-day laissez-faire bureaucratic confined fate or predetermined? Based on the perceived analytical parameters outcomes running cross tabulations to seek spurious connections of post-election agonizing truth of fifty-percent population behavioral disfigurement our lives are in flux subject to psycho physical sociopolitical invasive intrusive institutional surveillance mandated by white military paranoid psychopathic monomaniacal freaks unseen possibly heard constant scrutiny of all they own operate lease designed to regulate for dark purposes all they believe is their birthright to ultimately utterly control absolutely. Can't say I'm right here also my grief, I can't say I'm wrong! Seems predetermined covers it. Can't say for sure.

Ok, soooo with a spaceship like the Solar Power Molten Core Mass Thermal Electromagnetic Field Energy Exchange Dynamics spaceship the flight from here to Jupiter moons would be so quick fast and giddy up hurried more comfortable than a posh plush Air Overnight Grandma and Grandpa could make da trip wit da chillen the whole Familia. How 'bout dat Grammie's hop a stumpin' an' rumpin' jumpin' on Jupiter Moon!

I start to address the absence of subtlety entrenched exhaustion a weariness juxtaposed by saturation of press coverage of two pandemics. Egregious repetition screeching synopsis of death reports inadequacy ineptitude inability to salvage either sick patients or our gutted remains of American institutions. Dreary for inane lack of redeemable proselytes needed to temper man's inhumanity to man recuperating operational transitional traditional norms for bureaucracies. I feel like I am being used abused misused given up for dead lives stagnated by psychotic asymptomatic mentally disfigured monomaniacal murderous minion. Did no one ever think in all these years that a greedy loudmouth whiny-ass crazy white fool would not want to give up perks of power the presidency and think to install a failsafe act to stop the noxious loathsome deteriotive misuse of the Executive Branch? Sure needs it!

Ok, guys, the undaunted failure is panicked about intractable inevitability of his impending ruination as a regurgitation of the Executive Branch perhaps he can be enticed goaded lured influenced pried with money to leave right now even giving him explosives to blow mo shit up to hasten his departure free up our government currently stymied. Worth a try, he is a fiend fo cheddah and mo cheddah and mo cheddah. If this doesn't work try repeat procedures more poofy for the 1st lady failure.

Bottom line Boris and Natasha should go now back to Mother Russia.

Ok, how does the Solar Power Molten Core Mass Thermal Electromagnetic Field Energy Exchange Dynamics craft maximize universally provided Electromagnetic light dark matter field energy grids the superform is interior and exterior design engineered using thermal superconductive biomolecular microprocessors transfer conductive enhancers effectually aligning cosmic field grid densities nucleated beyond fusion a Charged Particle transversing time and space. To quote a phrase, "Hold on to your butts"!

Time to pencil into annals of American history anal Trump psychotic chaotic asymptomatic mentally disfigured monomaniacal psychopathic Mass Murderer not from the visionary presidential heroic leadership traditional to the office but for the dismal abysmal chronicle durationally malevolent malicious purposeful failure of service to the people what he was elected for. He seems hellbent to shenanigans wantonly destroying everything in his path. Why scorch it all then try to win again 2024? Unless you plan to walk on bones of the deceased desecration of societal remains survivors condemned to death by labor claiming hegemonic supremism. The moral Arc of History will bend in the direction of trumps accomplishments Cowardice and Mass Murder. Note Adolf Hitler still has followers.

If there can be no new low how low will Trump go? How low is low as can go when with each inconceivable extemporaneously lower low they go nonetheless subterranean lowering unfathomably limitless finding skullduggery appetizing chicanery worthy of praises maniacally grandiose. Americans suffer more intensely each passing minute desperation is prevalent the norm resulting from Presidential displays of morose deadly reoccurring capricious behaviors gauging out all of our eyes.

1st Lady must've colored dyed his toupee just before his news conference declaring Trump winner BS in front of cameras his face showed dye trickling down both sides of his face he looked like orange-white man bleeding black shoe polish Rudy Giuliani. Wow!? Wow! WOW!

Rachel Maddow called the riotously hilarious calamity of orange-white men and women faces covered with thick heavy shiny glowing makeup rouge Cover Girl sparkling sheen Giuliani bleeding black shoe polish the *Star Wars* Bar Scene!!! Kudos applause she owns brilliance bravo.

I have never seen such a blatant Lily White grandiose spectacle as the wealthy necrotic smelling of Trump death and decay publicly expose ignorances as intelligent banter, fabricate felonious senseless cult falsehoods, satiation of mutilated confused absence of mental capacity, rampant incompetence, lawless insurrection aimed at radical means to influence weak minded to support the preemptively foreseeable Trump anathema of a fetid coward and mass murderer destroying everything and most everyone. We must install Executive Branch measures to prevent future episodes of white man Failure to Launch!

In a way I can see why in a white society that viewed the American people as frivolous thus removing the popular vote as an option and installation of the Electoral College the white power Ace in the Hold diminishing stifling people's power. It follows suit that a white born of privilege would use the similar irrational paranoid psychopathic thinking historically prevalent used consistently to quell power to the people. The current functions of voting for leadership worked so well it represents desirable change from untethered racially motivated extremes to acknowledge freedom in the voices of the people. Z Trump including Z Trump minion just learned "we won't go back, we go forward." Look at the Orange-White Man's Face?!

Never seen a more sinister goofy orange-white obvious crony stooge looks like his head is also still covered in shack wank having just wriggled out of Trump posterior. See for yourselves look enlarge the photo Giuliani laughing stock of the planet. Not necessarily unexpected!

Can you see it? Giuliani in the proverbial royal headgear of Trump majesties "Medieval Court Jester."

Right bleepin' now it's about time for all news coverage no matter tendency to report nonsense to make an about face no more pussyfooting meet the charging bull head on hit him/it right between the horns of his cowardice, seditious insurrectionist gorging uncontrollable whale of a vain greed ridden narcissist by being in yo face direct every fantasy exposed as fiendish bile having migrated from essential stomach regions to abnormal flooding in the brain convoluting capacity for intelligent reasoning not saying disaster, death, dying and more dying, closures, collapse, work stoppage, no hospital anywhere with capacity to meet minute-by-minute increases in emergencies not just daily far more intensely cynosure unparalleled urgency a worldwide humanity crisis. We cannot wax hippie here pouncing on each and every real or remote opportunistic chink in the armor of the New Right-Wing Republican Fanaticism to expose it as Republican Party

Acute Diaper Rash of the mouth and derriere providing verbiage triage emulsifying party open sores, oozing wounds, dressing bandaging exemplifying healing philosophies to redirect the inching for a scratch knucklehead dipshit performances enticement to embrace responsibility. If that doesn't work a good slap in the face.

Tick tock tick tock tick tock time is a flyin' people are crying, fryin', painfully dyin' y 'n becausin' enemy of the State rampagin', burnin', tramplin', crushin', trashin', smashin', breakin', takin', rakin', "n the embodiment of all the hope dreams promises of the American people much like Godzilla Godzilla Godzilla Godzilla.

I want to let you in on my secret the Solar Power Molten Core Mass Thermal Electromagnetic Field Energy Exchange Dynamics spaceship because design features enable various magnetic field grid bonding trans-interactions resulting charged particle flight enhanced by ununpentium generated modulation dynamics engages spatial folding by transversing manmade ship propagated navigable singularities field forces accommodate both time travel and dimensional travel. You can be in 2, 3, or 4 places at the same time and speak to yourself proving it. You could visit those lost to you and the world or see what is coming ahead. I think when this happens rules inviolable will need to regulate sensible use of this awesome power and responsibility. I think when we achieve this we will be joining a interstellar galactic community of civilizations each hoping wondering if we could, should, would rise to be Civilized in the eyes of all who see.

Movie Tomorrowland George Cluny fantasizes a technological device using little-known theoretical perceived energy called Taction particles seldom witnessed slowest speed is faster than light normative beyond light speed natural to its environment. Movie harnesses power to create a platform in a surround visual arena wherein using a Taction Dialer they can see, be, anyplace, anywhere, every where. Problem chasing this pipe dream at our current rate of tech development it will take 900 years to detect it another 2-300 years to observe measure record then more to possible exploit convenience. Solar Power Molten Core Mass Thermal Electromagnetic Field Energy Exchange Dynamics spaceship does everything now 2-10 years by year 25 we can have families farming Mars and the Jupiter moons.

A race between the commonly viewed TV starships using either fission or fission or anti-matter conversations for their warp drive and the Solar Power Molten Core Mass Thermal Electromagnetic Field Energy Exchange Dynamics spaceship being warp drive presuppositions idealizes a manmade unique environment allows circumnavigation of laws of physics to go beyond light speed. The Solar Power ship may not achieve beyond light speed bit wins the race by spatial folding combined with use of navigable singularities in between folds providing shortcuts though sub or micro space without the contaminating features of dirty reactors creating lasting contaminated warps though space.

It's not beginning to look anything at all like Christmas all the dead long COVID-19 day death toll 195,000 Trump maniacally espousing in his letter Santa Claus royalty please make the Election and all those who did not vote for me or swear loyalty disappear go away be not counted Must be all for me see, Must be all for me see.

The United States can now proudly exaggerate boast about one-fourth of all COVID-19 cases are here each day death tolls increase currently 195,000 climbing higher each every minute similar numbers influence our deaths compared to the world. This did not have to be, it is a byproduct of ruthlessness cruel white hedonistic glutenous effort to devour all American life reject freedom for autocracy splayed pride patriotism gutted by irascible arrogance haughtiness indescribably diabolical unique to Trump control of Republican ethics. We have much to fear as it seems more dismal premonitions rip apart potential futures lives tossed in a sea of failures building like hurricane forces blowing cross the land bodies strewn flung against the shores mass carnage tornadic destructive outcomes we are helpless to defend ourselves against the unseen enemy pandemic or conflicted Trumpdemic.

Two pandemic cabin fever does not wax or wain serendipitous. Amalgamations derived from mass accumulations of morbid gloomy forecasts of seething impending ruination our doom racing towards us unrelenting unstoppable juggernaut caustic eroding every human assertion that our future chances are sunny and bright instead we seem to be fumbling in the dark unable to see or prevent the immensely ominous forecast of Trumpdemic instigated killing of each other to prevent being killed by someone else a dire consequence of surreptitious conspiracy to much like Pinky and the Brain Try to Take Over the World.

Irony playing out in public view real time the Trumpdemic instigator who has openly cursed everyone on earth including newborns those just conceived verbally brandishing loser as a foil and slashing slicing dicing trouncing egos under his feet like a Titan as raging raving chaos is now being tamed literally decoupling Trumpdemic legal cases all losing including the biggest clown show ever by his bumbling legal team led by Rudy Giuliani sweating black shoe polish talking crazier than dysfunctional Trumpdemic now biggest loser of all time. Payback is a bitch here well deserved. Take solace in the fact he only has 59 days left to blow mo shit up.

Time to prepare the way for the departure of his highness and entourage from the People's house open any old sarcophagus break out the sarcoplasmic embalming fluid don't bother to heat it room temp fire up the Munsters' Hearse wake Herman using lightning bolts we need a chauffeur tell Grampa we got to blow up grow up leaving a big wake quake fitting of Trumpdemic the flatulence cautery spewing from his Trumpcated reticular biggggg fattttt asssss.

All Hail the King Trumpdemic the Flatulent He Who allowed it to flourish!

What price did we really pay? Millions of Americans held prisoner between the proverbial rock and a hard place amidst two pandemics. One a viral agent hellbent on destroying more than Bubonic plague in Europe ta other Trumpdemic a Russian agent Presidential facade working on behalf of the kremlin brulee packin' punked pussy Putin to dismember this Democratic republic enslaved masses spoon-fed hypnotized by lies superimposed over morbidity reconstruction of the American dream emphasizing swallowing acquiescence to dictatorship Trumpdemic the new Republican Botox. That's one hell of a price to pay sacrificed all of our lives!

All these efforts made to stop State certifications of votes frivolous lawsuits one after the other. Now if someone is interested in really do a solid for America and Americans have the Trumpdemic itself Certified as a fucking madman and send him packing with the men in white uniforms to any Loony Bin with thick steel locking doors.

The Trumpdemic aftermath proportions of unrecognizable distorted realities wholly bleeding us dry of everything all we live for life love happiness friends futures death with dignity health education welfare freedoms cherished missed longed for worship recreation spring activities endless summer charity mo blessed tolerance of human frailty inadequacies holidays real Thanksgiving real Christmas Happy New Year's I'm dying, I'm dying, I'm dying to say He is Gone Forgotten Marred Defeated Pummeled Shredded Plucked Pried Torched Inundated Derupted Demolished Axed Torpedoed Bombed Deceased Entombed Cursed Expelled Regurgitated Exposed Discredited Disabled Repulsed Restrained Contained Exterminated Say Halleluyah.

As human beings we incur images challenges involuntarily accept responsibility for caretakership of our nurturing vital galactic community shelter Terra Firma lifeline lifelong occupancy in the Goldilocks Zone mother nature to us all maintaining future promise the greatest yet to be observed by humans limited by our inability to travel off world without stumbling over ourselves to visit in our lifetimes eyes on other worlds wonders of the known Universe just beyond the reach of mankind struggling coping with inherent elemental unrestrained greed larceny black-hearted deceit malicious ambivalence unconcerned with the suffering undeterred by helplessness hopelessness despair scarcity misunderstood obfuscated dangled intrepidly withholding opportunity due to perverted aspersions to publicly shared prosperity except for the Elite Chosen Few or people with a lot of empty space between the ears!

As a nationwide 2 pandemic family we are preparing one of the most historical celebrations of our founding communal Thanksgiving. Let us again cherish this time shared with friends family maintaining vigilance against the murderous virus seeking a place at all of our tables and equivalent murderous Russian agent and cohorts try to prevent food stuffs from getting to our homes. Find solace in the extraneous little anticipated by product of both demics unexpected welcomed inspired by our desperate struggles to save each other including Him he who allowed it to flourish Love is now more of a national dedication more Lifting as We Climb. Peace.

I like the potential offered by a Smart device such as the Solar

Power Molten Core Mass Thermal Electromagnetic Field Energy Exchange Dynamics spaceship Smart Gel as a coverage layer biochemical molecular bonding allows manipulation alterations for instance paint the wing of a 747 let it dry then you can fold it bend it crunch it into any shape put it in your pocket take it out let it unfold then bolt it in to fly. Go to a liquid oxygen waterfall on Venus falls are 4 times taller than Everest Smart Gel bodysuit you can fly down those falls waxing poetic you can swim in rapid currents 1200 mph in a liquid oxygen or hydrogen methane river you could erect the tallest swing ever a bask in astral awe bliss talk about feelings of accomplishment. Be the first on your block to brave bold new thinking discovering as I do it ain't new just right straight clear focused where it should be not perverted by desires for avarice. As Bob Dylan put forth, "The times they are a-changing." Rightfully so.

Trumpdemic voracious insatiable hoggish esurient edacious gourmandizing devouring everything it can see smell hear or touch unending torment horror in perpetual motion accomplished in catastrophe motion picture cinema visual blow up scenario style actors 2 pandemics competing to see which can pile up more numbers body counts cause more devastation utilize death depravity as an excuse for scarcity the obfuscated dangled reason mostly given for socioeconomic spiral decline cloaked by confusion but unable to hide the racially motivated perverted aspersions to publicly shared prosperity now made ever so intrinsically apparent by Him he who allowed it to flourish and his wolfish provocateurs.

Biden approved by popular vote by the people electoral college win combined we forge ahead characterized by cabinet selections demonstratively professional in verity expressive epic demeanor not hugging President-Elect Biden not swearing loyalty to him but overture to the people service honor dedication patriotism ethics morals values once again appreciated whistle blowers applauded respected military revered service honored government multitasking on all fronts including watching their backs for Him he who allowed it to flourish moving to checkmate 2 pandemics refill the Trumpdemic drained swamp undo all the don'ts of government mishandling move mass vaccinations reopen state economies open schools businesses back to business knockout remaining hospital cases lower daily infection rates overall death rate reductions redo our foreign policy fix mistakes of environmental legislation respond to global warming threat lots to do just to try to regain a lost normalcy we took for granted which may never be seen again for a long while nonetheless Biden presidency will need to be persistent insistent persuasive resilient guarded reticent open minded willing to encourage enable people power listen to constituents work with EPA, BLM, Women's rights orgs, protect immigrants fix immigration laws, LGBT liberation, increase minimum wage protect voter rights, lot of stuff on the plate to get done little time to work accentuate the positive go go go go go epa epa arriba arriba epa epa arriba arriba muy pronto rapido! Quick fast and in a hurry!

We acknowledge time for a change in government Biden brings back the American facade but cabinet selections demonstratively professional pacing to reestablish fleeting status quo leave something to be desired in the futures of progressive Democrats with all the idealists that sacrificed their judgment to commit to Biden camp with so much to do in do little time ultra-conservative efforts to fix America may stifle progressive sociopolitical gains alienating voters whose ornery trepid disenfranchisement may precariously pose possible obstacles to Biden reelection. Progressives, BLM, LGBT, Women's rights, Corporate hogging to rout out diseased, Raise Minimum wage, California tax shelter for Homeowners Rewrite for Fair Tax Codes, Taming the ruthlessness paramilitary murderous Police departments nationwide, Reorganize prisons, Fix corrupted Criminal justice system, Legislation to reduce failures in the Congress and Senate, trash Trumpdemic Space military branch don't take our insane inane visible failure of the human condition war into future space exploration it may be a disastrous enigma only common to Earth, less commonly used lies to obfuscate the real reasons for American reluctance to detach from perverted aspersions to publicly shared prosperity cultivating in the greatest society on earth a poor under class trouncing the real American dream opportunity for all. Let's hope it's not here we go again not more of the same American dream out of reach.

Here's what I was trying to say with that previous schnorsenkruggle possible our fix is to be such tight asses 'cause we know we got punked by the biggest loser tight ass but becoming bigger tight assholes is not the fix apply appropriate idealistic healing salves generously to affected aggregate areas of our society and culture trampled those forgotten to us invisible needy suffering through no fault of their own.

Ok, ok, ok, I have attended trash parties where in a tenant has been forced to move by greedy obscene Landlords last week in the residence to be vacated is nonstop partying but the last night demolitions rowdy raving raging tearing the place up vendetta for presumed contractual mistreatment smashing windows doors cut in half counters sculpted toilets planted in the middle of bedroom walls couches bolted to the ceiling leaving everything demolished. I know what to expect the apocastrophy Trumpdemic the flatulence is ripping skatt up tearing skatt apart pardoning skatt hiding amongst his skatt antique treasures of our nation absconded with as if taken from room compliments of a hotel skatt whacked public appearances skatt nuthin' else talking out the side of his neck. Get the fuck on, you skatt rat bassard.

Thanksgiving best wishes to everyone. We are blessed our family even with such troubled times have plenty for our tables fortunately but multitudes millions are struggling. We commit to making these struggles successful in improving quality of life for more to enjoy.

I guess with limitations humans bound by physical conditions creating urgencies shaping life's universal path overcoming challenges forging new dimensions of growth struggling now with apocastrophy so remotely unknown to pursuing efficacy bewildering phenomenal aspersions vehemently bulldozing first our entrustment unimplied permission granted by the people to be governed then atrocious abandonment relentless neglect of the government protections culminating in the scenes we awaken to the world over involuntarily evoking fear deep shock dread terror consternation realization that it is infinitely worse than ever thought possible ashes ashes ashes all around us we breathe it we are standing in it ashes polluting our lives lungs homes the world burning around us while the wolves fiendishly pursue preying on our traditions the pack Russian agent Him he who allowed it to flourish senators congress corporations elected politicians wealthy greed-driven meglohumans rejects of evolution destined not to continue in the Cosmic Calendar. We all in the world passing on DNA continuity have a lot of work to do to clean up Hoarders mess.

All that 2 say they fucked more shit up than we thought possible even for Trumpdemic.

You think now is moving slow Trumpdemic the flatulent still has a little over 50 days to throw Russian paint on everything even remotely American we watch sinking as a society and culture as red Russian leaves its mark visible from space. I have been in the trades for years paint removal is both time consuming expensive problematic requires extensive effort culminating in abundant finish detail now relegate reckoning stripping red Russian from our government house negotiating the Trumpdemic wolf pack Russian wannabes botch damage to the system will be slow perilous may in fact linger in repair indefinitely punishing our system and everything in it people are surprised now with no government stimulus or COVID-19 relief it may be indelible chronically torturously incompetent incompatible fix for the people may arrive mortally late tragic as it is already every man for himself. Not a time to drag our feet. Giddy up, yo.

We are the survivors so far of 2 pandemics both having launched the most devastating vicious attack on the world now fast approaching since the 1918 flu except here now it has happened in a shorter time frame use more sense than ever before to help yourself and others stay alive and well.

Light speed is it really necessary we seek the immediately impenetrable physical barrier? How long before we think the effort is not worth the cost? Solar Power Molten Core Mass Thermal Electromagnetic Field Energy Exchange Dynamics spaceship in Charged Particle Flights achieves the relevant velocity of electric current with exceptions for vacuum environment hyper accelerated transference energy field discharging approaches light speed I think it is just shy but energetic enough to ride recoiling space post initial bending. Most of the volume of light and dark matter will bend to the immense force of the ununpentium thermal field transmigration generators bends the bulk of space between origin and desired destination to a point at your location power of the folding space produces a wave bow ripple like surf minimum speed is required to immerse spaceship into the ripple staying enough in front of the focused point of terrestrial reshaping to course correct post astral ambient stasis. In this flight schema light speed is not needed just the travel speed provided by the mass of space including everything present in the transmigrated regions influenced by force of ununpentium gravity well. Now about the laws of physics in gravity well generated flight because time is shortened does it impede or hinder growth in flight diamond production? The diamonds grow in near the molten core mass not privy to shelter afforded the manned habitat pressures extreme tolerances would still take place diamonds should still be produced. With this extraordinary craft you can have your cake and eat it too.

So! What is it? Each day of our lives for weeks now infection rates death tolls climb soar to new highs we are beyond the total casualties of most wars now COVID-19 has out sprinted earlier public outbreaks 1918 flu poliomyelitis meningitis HIV/AIDS so far peskiest bug ever seen growing strengthening attacking unseen from all positions the entire world has been fighting on the front lines for more than a year real battles against spread only in the first 2-3 months then political espionage sabotage morose moronic purposeful abandonment of sworn by oath responsibility of constitutional protections criminal in concept arrogant in demeanor culpable in sociopolitical disenfranchisement of the American population instigated by Him he who allowed it to flourish Trumpdemic the flatulent cultivated by his twisted deviance perpetuated by unending vanity narcissistic precognitive asymptomatic psychiatrically fettered mentally disfigured monomaniacal murderous behaviors modeled by meglohumans transformed into wolves demonstrating proclivity for similar murderous criminal fetish and a willingness never seen to display this dank dark fettered fiendishness in public.

FOCUS

We are in apocalyptic nucleated rampaging raging All Out War against 2 pandemics no nation anywhere in the modern world was ready caught off guard us all now motivated to response readiness everyone everywhere anywhere combat engagement targeted focused right now tightening defensive strategies incorporating new methods to improve tactical rally industrialized production of irradiation plans executed to stem progress of human decimation organize unify. Win this battle onslaught see because no one is saying it yet but this one is a World-Ending Event moving faster to that goal every microsecond work must render ineffectual this threat vaccines can do the trick also possible something can go wrong virus mutates producing unintended unforeseen consequences blindness, asphyxiation, kidney failure, lung collapse, heart stoppage healthy viable scientific medical curative fixes soon or sadly Mankind May Be Facing Our Last Stand.

I'm gonna try by purposeful lucid diction to be honest verity unequaled unequivocally brutally blunt we are in greater peril than what is printed publicized reported photo documented take what you see and hear multiply by 4 every state is static numbed by knowledge we are not tracking COVID-19 adequately in any state the real number tabulations are much greater augmented by institutional backlash tantamount with bureaucratic inefficiency legislative impudence impugning front line heroic measures heroism on a scale unchallenged now by history ultimately facing Mankind's demise are the efforts by greedy meglohumans just enough to tip us closer to Armageddon premature unwarranted unavoidable tragically inevitable. Can we who are so wrecked as a unified culture succeed as so many times in the past with so many dead or badly beaten bruised in our society? There is only one acceptable answer our favorable recovery and outcome the other consideration bequeaths doom for all women and men not appreciatively desirably favorable as a preferred epilogue. Truth is stronger than fiction truth can set you free let truth be your guide truth is the door leading to the road to paradise truth is keep your fingers crossed we truly are successful in kicking ass a 2-pandemic ass whooping.

Shocking to express I missed something it has been staring me in the face like something around your feet making walking difficult but pay no attention seen not seen not witnessed. If it had been a snake? This place is has not been America not for 4 years and still is not the America I've come to call home. This disconnected distorted dire distressed demented discombobulated dreg is a real drag, man! What the flock? Shit! What the hell? I mean, is anyone else getting this does anyone else see this? Americans our country is gone stolen by a killer virus and proclivitous murdering meglohumans still trying to conceal the obvious whereabouts of their felonious deeds. America this country our home is sacrosanct recovery is prioritized necessity by any means necessary any all means using every heroic measure in this effort as Americans We Cannot Fail do we all understand We Cannot Fail.

Trumpdemic is delirious delovely delightful yes delirious delovely delightful yes demented disshoveled disconnected discombobulated done disgusted delively yes depressing defeated delonely yes defamed demoralized destroyed demonized delimited defunct detached disenfranchised tooo.

Poor Trumpdemic the flatulent Him he who allowed it to flourish seen by his own White House staff depressed ranting delirious angry shouting at times being compared to King George muttering, "I won, I won, I won," unable to assimilate or cognitively process incoming information duties of a Lame Duck quack whack loser POTUS meglohuman menace to this planet royally disturbed he hasn't been able to gather antagonistic support for lopping off peasants' heads, "Off With Their Heads no dilly dally Off With Their Heads," this being no longer considered not for humanitarian reasons has been discarded in favor of alternating public temper tirades visible panic attacks incontinence short-term memory loss fondling molesting his grandchildren sending tweets like a cow chewing cud summoning money from any dimwit already cheated still willing to throw they money away using proclamation to steal even dirt from the serfs so without character presence he has no standing trying to fix court decisions same no standing with his staff now content to identify Trumpdemic the flatulent as a Madman not to be confused with the hit TV drama a title well deserved as he should have saved the drama for his mamma!

How real does it get? How stark did does it have to be? A Front Liner tragic story of complex ranching loss "Oklahoma Nurse loses husband and mother to COVID-19, 3 days apart," to see and know this sadness loss horrible tragedy was preventable to understand this Front Liner has more family to protect as we all do throughout the world but she confessed we are in trouble overwhelmed under equipped to fight the onslaught of an age-old viral killer mutation of the Flu now practiced at mass killing of human beings sweeping over our planet now like a terrestrial funnel cloud generated from outer space we are losing but we cannot lose took much at stake we must face the music taps funeral procession 21 Guns Blue Angel Falcon Eagle Fly-by Amazing Grace Save me a Place mankind does penance for so many failures so many avoidable mistakes abuses misuse of caretaker responsibilities now focused 2 pandemics us all fighting for the very survival of mankind the earth can take care of itself fine for it is better off without us the time is now to reach deep down inside the endangered soul of humankinds odyssey if existence this is make it or break it. WE ALL WILL NEVER FORGET THIS DID NOT NEED TO BE!

Here's a humankind odyssey if existence for you unlike Odysseus you will make it home for

Supper. The Solar Power Molten Core Mass Thermal Electromagnetic Field Energy Exchange

Dynamics spaceship because of design features capabilities can take on a noble purposeful goal.

A challenge a boon for the living anywhere everywhere star chart mapping of known unknown.

Galactic travel to make future celestial navigations safe placing warning beacons at nearby

Black holes rendering them harmful anamolies avoidable crews manning such a venture.

This adventure could because of new technology crew becomes androgynous lifespans.

Extending to 500 years half a century is ample time to gather memorabilia for your photo album.

Collectable areas in your home. How 'bout that something to fight for drinks with little

Umbrellas in them. What a bon voyage!

I'm volunteering 'cause this stuff gotta be fixed we need someone serious to do it we need someone worldly to make judgements acumen seeking sane cure rational sensiscientific remedies acuity aligning our healing society and culture with lasting structural maintenance of viable legislative cohesion reinforcing the vibrant sociopolitical climate journey men won't be enough we need real developed tempered tried true seasoned professionally directed squadrons working in conjunction with the drive will power motivation determination winning parabolics outlined by worldwide parameters using a planform tested by simulations to get us outta this mess damn we're in a tight spot we should be targeting escape options damn we're in a tight spot no time to lose your head damn we're in a tight spot there's gotta be a way out gotta be a way damn we're in a tight spot we ain't a gonna give up damn we're in a tight spot Oh brother we gotta find our way out.

Hospitals in New Mexico are totally full Texas and other states bringing bin trailers to store corpses this is after over a year of direct battlefield confrontations numbers are going up increasing not decreasing lapse now in battle strategy gov. impaired incompetence obstructing COVID-19 medical lifesaver responses obstructing justice impeached POTUS Madman reeling now indiscreetly maniacal as they plan to conceal the most vicious efforts since WWII to overthrow US. Government using Russian assistance by POTUS request supported by Republican proclivitous murderous senators and congress wealthy entourage willing to lie under oath to sell us out seemingly without any negative consequence. When did it become acceptable fashionable to sell out your fellow countrymen? How did does this traitorous conduct rear its ugly Russian head here among so many patriots? Does patriotism have any meaning remaining or was it lost because of the deadly calamity of the war in Vietnam? Calamity a war just to save face no military objective where bombing strategies led to Agent Orange killing our troops beyond the battlefield killing also futures for young Vietnamese women causing lasting birth defects contaminating their soil indefinitely killing us here with disgust disgrace guilt for monstrous actions displayed by the military culpable for this heinous corruption and the beat goes on. Stupid military moves in Iran Afghanistan Egypt Saudi Arabia Israel it never stops America meglohuman murderous bullies of the Planet Earth we have to tell someone. How else do you stop a bully? Take the John Wayne American example knock the bully down necessary or not use ethics healthy rational discussions of alternative behaviors one thing is clear here these bullies will require a joint effort at eradication they are squatting on the hopes dreams of worthy people that deserve more for constant toil than feigned empathy. We voted this creep in just like Germany voted in Hitler we brought this on ourselves now what do we see dead piling up "n piling up "n piling up "n piling up no end in sight no light visible at the end of the tunnel. Vaccine in the works will it be a real fix or a technical placebo while we are ravaged by incessant machinations chronic corruption.

Presidential pardons are now Red Light District obvious dismissal of criminal felonious corruptible actions deliberate law violations treated like the good ole boys club. How can any crime against the state or people be summarily dismissed? This is mysteriously wrong inane nonsensical there should be no one pardoning crimes that happened or those about to happen. No president should be able to write off criminal conduct not for others his family or himself pardon power is an unacceptable anathema.

Damn you that think we are in the best of all possible worlds. Damn you for inexcusable recklessness voting in a tyrant. Damn you for not being willing to seek the truth about the greatest current threat to humankind. Damn you for doing nothing to stop good decent Americans from painful agonizing suffrage lonely deaths. Damn you for selling us out to the highest Russian bidder. Damn you for giving away national security secrets which will harm us. Damn you for ripping off robbing stealing burglarizing absconding with American institutional wealth treasury wealth citizen wealth international foreign exchange wealth Russian oligarch wealth banking wealth real estate income tax return wealth. Damn you for rapping demeaning molesting women. Damn you for inherent uncontrollable perverted aspersions to people of color. Damn you for contaminating value consciousness behavioral morality. Damn you for juvenile recalcitrance phobia retroactive imbecilic constipation redirecting consternation humiliation depilating extenuating erection derived from office of POTUS so occupying the attention displaced previously held by reason break out the hose hit the son of a bitch with cold water get him it to snap out of it and let us get the show on the road.

This is normally beyond my range I have been able to now understand in Charged Particle Flights discharging may produce invisibility to the external observer as the Solar Power Molten Core Mass Thermal Electromagnetic Field Energy Exchange Dynamics spaceship interacts with dense electromagnetic dark and light matter energy field grids making it in essence the varied description of a quantum particle based on in laws of physics. It would travel in known unknown space time on a quantum level calculable internally by dynamics of quantum particle based physics and able to be shared on a multi-spatial relativity. Aww heck now you all as over my head as this is I tried.

Understanding here is a space case trying to 'splain a little more about space taste of quantum physics mechanics the Solar Power Molten Core Mass Thermal Electromagnetic Field Energy Exchange Dynamics spaceship can be hereto called a Quantum ship able to utilize quantum wave complex dynamics to travel into space. I incorporate an earlier discussion of manmade navigable singularities thinking it can be done much like charged particle flight instead of discharging emit a focused particle beam like a lightning bolt separating fabric of space use a static bubble field aversion generator to keep the space separated for variable distances exploited for travel convenience it's as if you can using opposing wave constructions riding the peaks of opposing wave amplitude offering stable singularity reactions. Offering workable means to maintain the singularity perhaps using excited thermal energy states of hydrogen protons or helium nucleated neutrons or benign black holes reduced mega force output more like the effect output that might come from something the size of earth moon not Jupiter the gas giant. The more contemplation of particle theory quantum law particles can exist in two states at the same time atomic subatomic particles electrons protons neutrons and wavelength features of aforesaid. This creates two operational universes with a definite boundary between the two research of known unknown in this boundary region may provide clues to unlock the bubble verses conducively relevant to human exploration exploitation mastery of quantum mechanics opening up the Universe just for us saying like Frank Sinatra come fly with me let's fly let's fly away or fly me to the moon and let me play among the stars let me know what's happening on Jupiter and mars in other words Living Large.

14 million lose income unemployment expires end of December and they are also victims of the system-wide underpayments countless millions more may lose lodgings and find themselves homeless food bank lines being impacted in every state. With the gov. purposeful starvation of resources they should anticipate increases in emergencies crimes as desperate poor struggling against contemptuous failure of government institutions the dark shady side of America peeks out from the subterranean abyss men women desperate dog-eat-dog allowing themselves to be used for income abusing themselves and their children in ways obscene perverted dismal downward spiraling in despair ruin we now see the belly of the beast and what a monstrous beast this is. Maybe we should all ask Martha and Snoop Dogg go help!

Mo space case tryin' to 'splain mo space taste a navigable singularity visually may resemble in space the actions of a storm kinetic energy static tornado funnel cloud excited by vortex winds in space vortex waves maintaining an open vortex like singularity active and stable enough internally to accommodate safe navigations within the vortex wave phenomena is closer to current representations of wormhole theories.

Ok, I've heard enough so many doctors reporters nurses front liners politicians say in response to a question Are you able to see the government helping at this time of desperate need White House is radio silent POTUS just lying dog faced cheat lying still poddy mouth about winning Ga Arz PA MI all bald face grift right in front of cameras 45 minutes of the most twisted cows ass smelling lies POTUS if proud of nothing else can take a victory lap in the fat person cart most lies of any public servant in any country on earth even outdid Kim Jung illin' pussy ass Putin China Saudi Arabian prince most lies in history for any servant of the people of all time. Comments are Trumpdemic behavior is mind boggling shocking panicked deluded biased desperate cynical caustic volatile fanatical tyrannical edgy. Are they kidding? Did they really expect different? If so, why? He has always acted like an ostrich with his head up his own ass now a lame quack whack duck his wide load big root ass is in all our faces. Motherfucker is ass out.

What is it about The Big Man in anglo culture? From the earliest pilgrim settlements throughout massive European immigration clashes with indigenous populations ongoing active influence in the transformations of colonialism migrant dominance of communities social cultural philosophies throughout the industrial revolution classically illustrated in the motion picture John Wayne image Wall Street Wolf similar to the Mooch Anthony Scaramuzzi portrayed by Leonardo DiCaprio a nationwide multiculturalism and still this image is imprinted in the regenerative soul of a nation that should age like a fine wine instead imploding collapsing in on itself like being swallowed by a black hole white aggrandizement voluminous pollution venial insidious nefarious petty perverted proselyte personalities driven to homicidal madness incapable of the act of caring or concern for others these are human qualities maybe our misfortune Meglo-Dehumans are not able any longer because of obsessiveness over murderous goals to embrace love happiness compassion friendship paradise truth equity value moral respect appreciation accomplishment honor dedication justice approval alliance partnership community only their narrow minded haughty visions of White men purified by white is right birthright subjugating white women enslavement of all others inferior by not being white continuing to fool themselves into believing that because they can comb orange blond nasty looking hair much like "Cookie, Cookie, Lend Me Your Hair" Edward Burns of 77 Sunset Strip into a strange beach comber pimp pompadour kind of thing hanging over his lack of forehead like hair of the shaggy dog that bit him. How on what planet in what life could any sighted intelligence ever be deceived by these orange-white pork like nasty nasty nasty troglodytes say right?

China greatest continuing threat to freedom in the west expanding populations world power status international foreign exchange wealth expansionists wanting to take over more territory and bend the will of the Chinese people to communist extremism. We all know but put out of our minds about those inaccessible places secreted military or corporate big money research labs some of which too long ago as a matter of routine fact started down the forbidden dire dark contagious path of radical scientific ineptitude investigations into the fringe vicious unknown technical efforts be they chemical genetic sub atomic horror laboratories the mad scientists all over the world in places least expected definitively violating any code of ethics mutilations carnage body parts everywhere now China genetically wants enhanced Super Soldiers they are conducting experiments on human beings who have no refusal options in doing this research they open new pandora box threats usually kept contained it is not a stretch to be keen on the fact COVID-19 or stupidly referred to as the China virus is one of many life-threatening lab originated enigmas but this one escaped the confinement of the laboratory. In the dark ages Plague-infested European countries devastation of half the population in multiple laboratories original samples of the Bubonic Plague have been cultivated nursed fed given vitamins to study the most deadly contagion possible this is not all imagine Flu research or well-nourished Poliomyelitis meningitis the list goes on. We are toying with life ending viral threats supposedly preventative but the real goal here is to kill more people than anyone else easily. What a fucked up goal for any government to endeavor. The time is now to recognize we have a way out one chance it is here already established with international goals to benefit humankind world over the United Nations before it is too late turn control of military to them all nations relinquish strategic goals of conquest and focus like *Life Magazine* on the business of quality of good Life.

Quantum physics incorporates uses of calculations of probability study particle motions wavelength theories in the interaction between two universes predicting quantum outcomes. In the motion of a wave length study where might an electron proton neutron intersect with the wave amplitude influencing physical phenomena? Complex calculations into the known unknown universe provide insights to technical growth producing understanding to create microchips capacitors processors communications visual soon we'll developed holographic tech space venture. What was the probability of our survival of COVID-19 in January of 2019? What is it now December 2020? What will it be on January 20 very likely the first real day of sensible gov action in 4 years? What is the probability of survival given 50 percent of population are petty perverted proselyte personalities? We truly are far worse off marred offset by vague inuendo into all life is cherished here wrong it is not all of us sorry to say are really accidents waiting to happen moving much more rapidly now imposing haranguing herding hurling us all towards untimely circumstances. What is the probability you can take the pebble from my hand before I close it? When you can do this Grasshopper you probably will use probability to procedurally navigate predicting quantum universes.

Mo space case taste a Quantum ship probably within a calculable rational probability could perform an amazing feat you can surround yourself with yourself on a multi-spatial dimensional universally distributive quantum level eventually you could see you every place everywhere around above below. If you really haven't seen enough of yourself talk about full of yourself smile.

What it is? Apparent now blatant in your face machinations adherence to Republican proclivitous dismissive divisive dogma dark suspect wicked continuing disregard for social processes Band-Aid remedies commonly used to heal communities are not being allowed as we coddle a lifeless vengeful power mad incompetent purposefully just "standing in the way of progress saying mine mine mine everything is mine mine mine mine" reminds me of a Looney Tunes problem is cartoons are mostly harmless Trumpdemic aftermath is of massive deadly proportions he is being coddled when he should be cudgeled with a good piece of wood made in Louisville slapping sense into senseless don't cut it the bat would leave a mark time for Republican hold outs to stop licking the wide-load Trumpdemics big fat smelly asinine conflagrations and pay reluctantly more attention to they needy rich spouses who have been snogging the pool man or the gardener high maintenance needs not being met by Trumpdemic Republican cowardice minions. Tada Huey dueyfudyddd ha ha ha whohoo the world according to Trumpdemic minions. Now you know why it is important to use the Louisville Slugger to make lasting Republican marks.

Trumpdemic turns his brainless off and on like a light switch as he barfs up another one takes a dump on us y'all multi ton pats his rouse done facially sprays on his orange oil paint so he can shine like the sun Trumpdemic the mighty white master Trumpdemic be whites only way he wants it to be now who you the suck wants to see Trumpdemic the small win tall Fades "em all yeah you that don't want to see Trumpdemic drop the ball Fades "em all yes you that don't want to see Trumpdemic take the fall Fades "em all yeah you that you want to see Trumpdemic hands and knees crawl.

"A Promised Land," title of America's first black President's book. Title comes from a fifty-year-old speech by Dr. Martin Luther King expressing his belief that one day we all would arrive at The Promise Land. Obama being a University law professor would expose constitutional history law sociopolitical economic rhetoric inclusive of multicultural movements his derivation of A Promised Land. Dr. King in his book The Promise Land may have referred to more of a biblical inference driven theological derivation. Whatever you ascribe to both entail people of color latent arrival at venerated humanistic conceptual paradise. Let's face reality like the bitch slap in the face we all want to willingly serve the Trumpdemic in this the lifetime we have all come to know and love. Trumpdemic and proclivitous petty perverted proselytic personalities nefarious prevalent primal pompous permanently permeates human primate culture we cannot escape this at least we have a rough idea a handle on approximately how many unfortunately are ok with denying the rest of us acknowledgement of a cultivated more gracious style of life live let live I mind my own business you mind yours do unto others whatever we can do to help how can we be of service is there something you need shelter in the cold shelter for our souls instead of in the heat of the sun a man died of cold.

A follow-up of preceding dialogue paradise is out of the question here due to the K rails placed by Trumpdemic-like Meglo-Dehumans that have been stopping progress in favor of traitorous attempt at American Gov. overthrow selling us out to Russia oligarch wealth. The Quantum ship I propose could in a short time provide a new home paradise for those willing to shed the bonds constraints of years of oppression and brave a new world where life can achieve exactly those dreams we have fought so hard for so many centuries only to come up short so close due to modernity so close you could almost touch it but the realization is we will detect a beyond light speed tacion particle before paradise is ever revealed here.

"A seven-layer cake of lies," CNN reports channel 11 other all right media distorts reality writers corrupt twist the truth only a few in those sources speak truth to this foul stench-ridden Republican power grab a POTUS that is illiterate does not read incompetent only seeking self-aggrandizement using resources of the office to presidentially grift money from dimwits that can't see beyond this nationwide scam largest grift scope ever witnessed from a contemptuous murderous maniacal madman willing to kill us all including those in foreign countries like Ukraine Afghanistan Egypt Iran London France Spain he's murdering there also we seldom go there beyond heinous beyond maligned beyond malignant beyond insidious beyond venial beyond conspiracy mongering culpable visceral denialism inflammatory inciteful feigned detachment from reality in fact focused on stealing everything from everyone even this is not enough there is still the continuing power grab. If a 2-pandemic daily debacle is not enough to keep you sick lasting misery associated with efforts to prevent grift shyster contamination from getting in our mouths. What is the probability our nation will endure this sustained attack of Trumpdemic Republican marauders and reroute us away from corruption fueled atrocious conditions? I think the odds of a good recovery decrease daily a fix moves farther from reach. I saw the corruption of the news reporting years ago when George Putnam ran Channel 11 broadcast like a mob syndicate a departure in the 70s, 80s from conventional reports this anal Republican has been noxious loathsome deteriotive ever since. With the change about to come maybe we need a real hard rain agonna fall to be able to wash away the chronic fettered stench the Republican cronyism vomited Trumpdemic.

Any American committed to a dream also has to bauk same dream is shared by Republican proclivitous perverted Meglo-Dehumans with an insidious devious radical. Continuing to make irrational attempts to subvert Democratic processes into fixing Election results and since Nov. 3 not facing reality is not a luxury that can be afforded being 2 colossal pandemic crisis negates any stifling petty party redundancies mandating optimal coordinating of emergency disaster responses to slow the spread and now mobilize nationwide life-saving vaccine dispersal. I haven't seen this government so stupid or stubborn since Macarthyism machination was using Communism and The Big Red Scare to destroy lives and democracy in the name of patriotism. Frustrating that our country has to deal with this Trumpdemic cynicism feeding them their baby bottles changing their crap filled diapers tying up valuable time and personnel a task that should fall on each of their parents for handicap care.

Here's one for you "Microwave energy suspected in mysterious illnesses of American diplomatic core." When asked who has this technology Russia China North Vietnam Iran Iraq Syria Now why do they suspect use of this weapon is limited for some strange reason to gov. . agents do they politely grant immunity hell no they have been targeting our citizenry for decades hardworking men and women attacked machination from their childhoods unable to avoid resist a dire challenge immoral unwarranted fiendish in scope something the victim can describe in the respect of symptoms but can provide no verifiable proof like being attacked by poltergeist would bet your proof of this apocalyptic atrocity is the overcrowded mental institutions with mild or major Schizophrenia used typically to explain the unexplainable. Use against citizens is vile but spreads potential for disruptive chaos tearing us down as a nation machination little by little destroying lives unable to retaliate as the menace can hide behind distorted corrupted nationalism as world conquest has not stopped but has become accepted like nomenclature.

Ok, ok, ok, I've had just about enough of this escapist retarded jerk pootenanny crap. I volunteer for the good of us all for the cause for the need for the amenity for the children which I request please cover their little eyes and ears reiterate I volunteer volunteer I say the America I know knew thought I knew but maybe no I volunteer to hit I repeat to hit him where it hurts to get his flatulence out of the way of whatever progress beyond this conniption.

Kind of cool to start speculative theoretical mental ambulating from my origins as riding the waves ripples of tidal life supporting forces bonding then with the morning sunrise the electricity one could felon the water a connection earth sun sky universe now a merciful glimpse at understanding the Quantum ship can open up the Universe in much the same way moving as particles transmigrating quantum physical boundaries coincidentally interacting with galactic wavelengths riding ripples of the fabric of space time not the Silver Surfer but close as I can get bonsai.

Man, I know it's always overwhelming gonna be a crowded here on lovely Earth but the sinister lunacy witnessed unchecked caustic undiminished about Herd immunity population thinning culling proletarian mind control brain washing genocides wars holocausts epidemics as I sit in my residence power out now over eight hours dark now used to it because of living in a fire zone power outages always cognizant of inconvenience when coming from work daily started collecting lanterns for indoor use everywhere I went to now using a small generator. I can power essentials light frig microwave Smart TV far removed from days of The Croods using cellphone can watch stuff all over the house but still 2 pandemics deaths a gettin' higher every day can't go nowhere can't see nobody safely we more necessarily tragically undesirably kept apart nearly intolerable everything closed up holidays cancelled sadly Regal theaters have closed now as I virtually sit in the dark can't help but wonder the path is this dark now only the beginning gonna be much much worse than humanly palatable.

Respect props go out in a solemn salute to one of the nation's most valuable citizens worthy of being recognized a hero aviator legend General Chuck Yeager military decorated Medal of Honor recipient test pilot broke sound barrier 1947. I had the inconceivable amazing honor of meeting the departed General Yeager at California Aviation an FBO I was employed at the Santa Monica Airport he would fly in and out affiliated with their agency. I remember eyeing him with a great deal of respect admiration as I was looking at an American war veteran a Legend in his own time a privilege distinction earned well deserved I salute him whatever his personal camber Rest in Peace, Sir.

Boy, do we need to put a real permanent fix on the obvious federal legal blunders that allow a clueless derelict to on camera in public record bully brandish contemptuous pressuring machination threatening lawmakers to overturn Election results dispose of Biden victory to favor Trumpdemic instead this is a felony you and I would be arrested. This flaw in government machinery is a priority law must prevent future similar abuses of white aggrandizement in the Executive Branch for the sake of all of us who don't want to have even any knowledge of this Trumpdemic skittish juvenile diaper-rashed infantilism.

Power outage yesterday kept me from the usual barrage of war movies played every year since in remembrance of December 7 war on two fronts the US victory commemorated in infamy John Wayne recruitment jump starting Americans to rally patriotism unequaled in history. Today in Europe Pfizer vaccine dispersal starts for citizens called VJ Day referencing WWII ends amazing efforts to create a lifesaver formula to put down COVID-19 as a pandemic and render it a harmless tribble (furry creature cute insatiable appetite) props to professional medical scientific researchers as the production of vaccine in record time now hope it works with minimal harmful side-effects. Painful as it is to say despite little time remaining in the White House Trumpdemic is likely to linger every day seeing this horrible creature evokes an involuntary reaction to hurl sadly Pepto-Bismol is now a coping mechanism I feel your pain. None of us deserved this dickhead ass backwards menace none of us.

Glad to say with the rapid development of a vaccine for COVID-19 we may be embracing a needed technological leap forward as stifled as this treachery has left us there is still time for mankind although in drastic recovery to transcend the bonds of extremism ineptitude and lunge forward against the tide of hopelessness emerging vanquished as victims achieving beyond expectation brilliance well deserved. Let's get there, everyone. Bravo!

Talk about retrospect the sheer odds of a youth started out as African-American living in a family unit each day eating a hearty breakfast listening to Captain Mack Shumaker flying a news helicopter reporting on the weather being a good day for test pilots to break the sound barrier. They would prepare listening audience for the phenomenon heard city wide often hearing the name Chuck Yeager ready up to hit the streets wide open only after realizing the sordid reality of Venice Beach after hours to wind up at the Santa Monica Airport a ground crewman Gunnell Aviation then California Aviation where I fueled helicopters CHP, LAPF, LAPD, UCLA Emergency Medivac often hot with blades rotating. I was formally introduced to General Chuck Yeager one evening arriving to work I spoke to him shook his hand proudly jealous you might say I had just started private pilot lessons I was standing next to a living legend of aviation war ace veteran couldn't escape feeling embarrassingly inadequate now years beyond that fateful introduction I am fortunate to theorize advance put forth a new rational. A Quantum Craft elite in design planform construction and Conceptual features able to traverse spatial fabric bound by Einstein Universal Theory of Relativity and Unified Field Theory matter bending space causing time to slow down so light can always accomplish 186,000 mph universal constant. Time speeds up also slows down bending light is observable. Imagine the odds of being there to meet a seasoned great me just trying to make aviation greater in my meager way. To Infinity and Beyond!

Fission as I understand it is for want of a better description ideally is Cold Fusion. Fusion bombarding an active isotopic element particle to get it to split releasing the maximum optimal energy consuming over 90 percent of mass. Fission has to make the particle want to separate as in a natural avoidance an escape mechanism to flee collision or an expectorant particle action desirable quantum splitting motion to embrace the coincidental reagent in other words a particle that with the right coaxing is willing to capitulate without all the expectorant drama. I have to work out details. I am also paying attention to the Black Hole Singularity at its Apex trough time must literally halt light travel faster to breach Apex Boundary. What next reatomized molecular integration bonding? Nothing but light time standing still? In the White Room with Black Curtains at the Station!

So I'm thinking Fission is that elusive female attractive curvaceous sensuous fetching alluring out of your league beckoning irresistible and scientists keep going the show off route bombarding particles ever faster flexing muscles like Franky Avalon Beach Blanket Bingo movies routing head butts with atom smashers. What about using in this case romance an enticing particle aphrodisiac pleasant coaxing the reaction then using stimulating not bludgeoning ununpentium 360-degree surround activators gravity then accomplishing the wanton particle split and subsequent releases of nearly 99 percent of mass instead of everyone going the same path treat that particle like a Pretty Woman, Treat it like a Lady and it'll be Good to you. Do you know what I mean?

Also I suspect the answer to Black Hole Singularity crossing transforms all visible light heat mass into dark matter expanding the dark matter in the Universe and moving galaxies farther away from each other.

It seems now, Ladies and Gentlemen, as if we are in a movie our government has informed us, "We have been unfortunately attacked by a virus killing us all destroying our lives homes," much like Mr. Po on Briney Beach addresses Klaus, Violet, and Sonny the Baudelaire children orphaned by. We are facing a Series of Unfortunate Events virus killing like wildfire economic social recreational institutional shut downs political disunity lies machination cheating vicerous vindictive inciteful harmful rhetoric distrust of efforts to stem the constant chaos all of us wanting it to be over now right now seeking sanctuary. Baudelaires sought sanctuary when thrown into care of a murderous illegitimate relative Violet would tie up her hair with ribbon and create from junk accommodations. 2 pandemic knockout punch jabbing us all into different areas of the ring bobbing weaving to escape haymaker just as the Baudelaires used calm adolescent wit to escape death on the train tracks, Cousin Martha's tumbling house, death by Lachrymose leaches, being eaten by the Incredible deadly viper (a misnomer), avoidance of being trapped in a wedding plot to steal their inheritance. Trumpdemic imachinations are imposing attempt after attempt to permanently ingratiate himself stealing everything we have got including our underwear. We continue now as the Baudelaires trapped in a Series of Unfortunate Events. Recommendations evasive maneuvers immediately.

The loss of mass in fission splitting the nucleus with neutrons nucleus absorbs one causing a split until two particle nuclei different in atomic mass the energy released in the reaction is the loss of 1 percent of mass seen as explosive light heat radiation. Three new neutrons are created in each new reaction to maintain universal laws of physics constants each one capable of generating a new reaction thus enabling chain reaction unlimited energy for unlimited purposes. How to do this simply with household items next.

A little moment before workout. The Quantum ship I propose using Solar Energy ununpentium generated gravity well Electromagnetic Field grid dense energy quantum wave transfield migrations Molten Core Mass Smart Gel all nonconventional relatively new scientific areas like fission and fusion opening up new superhighways of intellectual strata ready to navigate assimilating knowledge facts as osmosis evolving despite opposition detrimental to successful outcomes.

Ok, the Trumpdemic shows out unbuckles his penis restraints pulls down his executive embroidered incontinence diaper turns around bends over and moooooooooons us all in the face on January 20 Biden Harris Inaugural Ceremony Trump machination calls on proud boys QAnon skin heads Nazi Aryan militia plus all the rest of the nuts to assemble to jostle the affair to violence never before witnessed in America the same kind of juvenile incitement before school kids fights or two kids in a neighborhood brawl. Anal Asinine Assout Asshole Ass Backwards.

Whoever wants to see the worst of a human being? Whoever wants to see or encounter the worst of anything? Who's with me in saying it is utterly intolerable to be faced with no choice between engagements in 2 pandemics? Why is it not apparent to any living being these stench-ridden foul subterranean mean lowering of apathy misers are a byproduct of ruthlessness self-hatred gorging on us our health happiness friendships frailty inadequacies short comings like Nosferatu? Why we should need to stuff our pockets, use leeches bloodletting poultices rabbits foot burn cense drink elixir root remedies because we are as serfs to outgoing administration and cohorts? Why must we continue to tolerate the intolerable? Is this the new harsh American permanent pressure cooker? If so, perhaps a retreat to interactive psych therapy will do the trick just what is needed! Yeah, Right!

Biden cabinet choices suggest he is keen conservatively focused on credentials prior job experience nonpartisan professionalism the addition of Susan Rice connotes practical extension of continuity of quality of leadership coming from the office of Obama stimulus to corrective regimen to fix the damage heal the injuries stop the bleeding perpetuated by POTUS Republican causal agent machinations. So much damage done so many casualties so many convolutions mounds of grief suffering ongoing mounting death tolls high positivity modern day dark ages a hard fix for any quality team no matter what capabilities has the plan been all along break more sshit up than ever before making it impossible to recover. Why all the Republican nonsense if the plan is to destroy it all? What will they salvage from Armageddon? With nothing else to destroy they will start on each other perhaps leading to an outcome much like the Easter Islanders. Ironic final outcomes for Republicans murderous savagery tribal conflicts cannibalism fitting end them eating each other.

There are laws against inviting violence for personal gain laws against any menace trying to abridge the voting rights of citizens on basis of race color previous condition of servitude sex age over legal 15th, 19th, 26th amendments require thus the serpentine snake-like low down dirty dog conduct by Trumpdemic the flatulent machinations including parasitic bloodsucking primate hoard infectious toxic noxious tepid appallamendous foul rank tyranny tolerated actions intolerable able to be acted upon by Congress as principally felonious premeditated conspiracy to overthrow the will of the American people conduct far more visible than Benedict Arnold more murderous than John Wilkes Booth all parties now directly competing with Hitler even worse the US for Hiroshima Nagasaki and Vietnam. I know for a goddamn fact I do not like to arise awaken to the smell of burning napalm damn now with this 2 pandemic crap killing us at a faster rate than me innepegs 'n all that can we just this one time Get it the fuck together use law to rescue us all from this lawless rabble.

The audacity machination the unmitigated gallstone callousidiousness the berating mockery of people guided Democratic processes depletive archaic seditious insurrectionist anarchy supporting facade lunacy barbarism amongst modernity annihilation of overwhelming credence undeniable verisimilitude reality if in fact existence resultant deductive reasoning of Election denial to grift public morbidly culpable chokingly derailed bats in the coup bustin' out da roof yo Cardi B he wants this ho he wants that ho yo shakin' his big fat ass so you will give him yo cash give him yo money give him yo money now he'll take yo money then throw you out that's right he'd even pimp out his wife wasteful depletion of scarce resources is more than heathen or criminal 56 lawsuits to overthrow Election results should be liable for lawsuit and a straitjacket at the county hospital. Right now.

Trumpdemic machinations voracious insatiable hoggish apocastrophy anathema wicked amity Supreme Court dropped a rock on he not a merry old man see ornery trepid cuss miserly executive puss by product of white rust oxidation of living unjust distrust abominous carnal primitive primal savage Precambrian regressive tribal bestial carnage where will it go from here anybody's guess caution suggestions lock away stuff you want to keep it's a new day vaccine on the way only 100,000,000 in the line afore me will it get here in time to save me of thee I see.

DEDICATION

One thing at a time. Status quo normalcy the usual pace of life here has been forced to change desperate efforts to get people to work together to face head on a common enemy are ill due to mistrust unrestrained opposition to curative dogmatic reason ideology directed to crisis containment remedy leading to universal cures. Problem as I see it typically everywhere anywhere there is the overall rush to mobilize but over time this diminishes efforts slow useful personnel fluctuates inevitability neglect resultant implication people go unserved some are left out. Not that slow walking to achieve goals is so unusual it's just that now life-threatening urgency is calling the shots 2 pandemics now massive suffering as millions do not have enough to eat this is a political problem for there is enough food produced. This is now a 3-pandemic crisis moving to 4-pandemic as money will factor soon and homeless population doubles overnight. I don't care who you are or what you are all about nothing here is a quick fix anymore the homeostatic resistance of our nation has been under attack the past 4 years being the most obvious indicator we are weakened national recovery has no choice but to be slow agonizing this is long-term foreseeable we cannot afford here to be complacent can't let our guards down throw status quo away no time to play or we will slowly painfully waste fade away.

Here's one for you the Quantum ship can do that what by physical laws physics says you cannot do but to do or not to do it can do from traveling at any speed to the observer this craft can come to a complete alto halt stop instantaneously with no further movements on any axis no pitch no roll no yaw no frontal or backward movement in defiance of Newton's Laws of Physics. No other movements either in nature or manmade lab can anything duplicate this phenomenon at least indigenous to earth however I have knowledge of creatures for careful lack of a better description I call them RFL as in Rare Flying Lifeforms I have enormous undeniable photographic proof over 1,000 pictures of their presence here in fact my Quantum ship understanding comes from over 5 years of observations of some of the creatures flight abilities observed stopping in midair on a dime and remain still over 2-4 minutes another I was absolutely blown away I experienced something rarely witnessed. I tried to explain to myself what I had observed I could only describe it as Charged Particle Flight I later worked out I had seen quantum mechanics at work then designed Quantum as a craft in the quantum world a particle or craft can exist in two states calculable by Unified Field Theory and appear at random coincidence. Even a crash dummy car on impact is not a complete halt the front impact mostly stopped but is moving omnidirectionally as the rest of the car is under centrifugal force moving to the wall Hancock came close stopping the train but there was still movements. I have come to this realization because I have seen it with my eyes I have also had to deal with the ugliness of self-doubt trepidation I had to work to explain the cunning intimidating unexplainable cultivating a careful consideration of having a powerful observant mind open to new truths awarenesses never regretted cautiously sheltered indelible mega wondrous.

If you think the poverty level here is horrendous now attention eyes front get ready you ain't seen nothing yet. The 4-pandemic knockout punch this whammy has crippled all normative options for labor related economic self-improvement causing lame stagnation impaired futures now fouled by life-threatening urgency to shelter in place largely alone with impetus to avoid gathering contrary to human nature we know holidays are shot looking to spring for some relief only to find like the desert herd off seeking water in a drought rains did not come they have to struggle on so do we have to swim forward against the current like salmon going upstream avoidance in our efforts COVID avoidance. As the dominant species here we are in a scrape we have to scrap our way out of it. This is not about good luck it's about getting back to quality good living.

Let's discuss Quantum ship practicality Universal remotes used commonly a variety of these exist operating operational appliances for convenience ships remote once activated paired with ships multifunctional super quasi quantum computer interfacing directly with ships systems the remote can promote your travel protective Smart Gel bodysuit this remote can transport to Paris leaving here as a quantum particle arriving as a quantum wavelength then materializing as a quantum particle as the wavelength exchanges places different than the matter stream concept of a transporter in the TV stuff more a matter of quantum mechanics crossing boundaries and thresholds. This feature holds another primary import a design element of the Quantum ship there are no entrance or exit hatches after inherent construction ship is impenetrable by any invasive means thus eliminating design flaw entrance exit is by particle exchange energy transfer. Captain 1st Officer would be outfitted with a biometric device enabled by subcutaneous surgical bond. Crew manual carry. Another thought one day Smart Gel bodysuit configuring will also enable limited flight capacity.

Does some of what we see regulating our daily lives seem a bit slow redundant impaired impeded starved choked inhibited pinched or is it really machination derailed tendency obsessive compulsive rectal retardation to control dominate suppress needs of the people by jerks like Meglo-Dehumans proclivitous perverted proselytic personalities murderous in attempt at American coup. Hilary Clinton casting her Electoral College vote today called for the dissolution dismantling of the College in favor of People's Popular Vote to fix these United States this must be done no longer is it acceptable to call a citizens vote too frivolous All Votes Count by Law put down the white godfather hold card Electoral College must be abolished as a responsible Educator prior to racism quelling my career I informed my eighth-grade classes of this being a necessary proper riddance of US gov. Disfunctionalism our social handcuffs chains bonds limiting our rights freedoms since 1776 quite long enough, don't you think? Jolly Good!

The mad dash the rush reckless hurry irascible push shove bash rash racing to get out front ahead of others lead out marginal impetus to outdo everyone to get to the front of the line break all the rules trample faces of those weaker needing it more because some just know they are special and deserve it for whatever twisted reason more. Vaccine is not crisis now averted it is in fact crisis just started "On Your Mark- Get Set- well, you know!"

The man called lame duck Trumpdemic the flatulent Him he who allowed it to flourish continuing machinations now has to fumble with Electoral College formally deciding Election results he waxes simpleton while around his imposing big fat stinking ass Republicans are jumping ship like rats escaping drowning fleeing abandoning the insanity Putin must have given the thumbs up to Moscow Mitch to recognize in a Senate statement the new President and Vice President elect. I don't think Trumpdemic the fat fuck ever had his sea legs he is off balance on a tossing deck seasick throwing his family overboard clinging to his golf clubs and the golf cart now sinking and the idiot is drowning as he wants to hold onto the golf cart sinking as well incapable of moving his lard through 18 holes walking desperation is now the name of the game as he feels he has more to destroy disable ruin deplete damage detonate deny dislocate derail delude running out of time to do it. His cognizance is distorted reality consistently delusional not the World According to Garp more a version of The Cat in the Hat take that in the final days he will swing flail his arms wildly at nothing fighting the sinister lunacy that is he even That Cat in That Hat can see.

There is a great big black hole at the center of our nation Trumpdemic the flatulent Him he who allowed it to flourish it is on a universal machination scale trying attempt at American coup still not done impending ruination laid out on our tables of traditions heaped onto our plates where we have taken time to lay out sufficient fixins appealing satisfying palatable pleasing usually but facing the oblivion prefaced by being sucked into the accretion disk beyond where time slows down the force of 126 Senators and 18 Attorney Generals rippling gravitational forces ripping apart matter for conversion to energy singularity needing to fuel fires of hatred fan jealousy contempt cruelty disregard for human suffering no defense against it escape will entail courageous tactical avoidance skills using means to provide an adept relocation of communicative ideological dogma enticing narrative breeding resistance generationally carving new paths outmaneuvering black hole clutches of the Trumpdemic the flatulent Him he who allowed it to flourish gravitating with the Senators Attorney Generals imploding collapsing in on the center of reason of which there can be no escape from like the massive holes in their hearts that cannot be filled.

Saving time has been a lesson learned. It started somewhere along the way the upbringing being reared by kinfolk beholding as family probably earliest attempt to grasp this meaning had to do with money time clocks working. A function of multi tasking independent episodes of a series of outcomes affectual in exquisite knowledge accumulation compilation an integral part of everyones life to be prompt. Efficiency expertise is learned behavior that being the case explanations of why so much time is wasted is enigma problematic puzzling as fallacious concentration on sociologist issues which find their way to reported news forefront publicized chronically as an intelligent international modern society we should have seen our way beyond these stymie calamities a long ago. Not the case we dwell on ignorance stubbornness buffoonery morose incognizance treated as commonplace as a modern culture we have not escaped being stuck on stupid no offense to any reader but our time culture world is really a trap inescapable we are all imprisoned any prison is detrimental. So what the hell is really going on? Why does so much here act to incarcerate? Freedom is ideology prefaced by value why spoil it? Man, talk about a lot of shit to fix.

News top story "Top Trump Appointee; We Want Them to Get Infected"! Now what in the Sam Hill? This is an outright admission by someone in one of the highest gov positions the envy of so many a career vaulter prestige bonafide credentials unparalleled to backslide split hairs behest tarnished mockery vehement behemoth bowls of visceral necromancy as they seem to do the equivalent of pray for our demise. They want us to succumb to lethal infection mortal contagion today 4200 deaths in CA over 16,000,000,000 cases US don't forget to factor in those numbers not reported as much as 50 percent higher over 300,000 dead in 8-12 weeks the unmitigated pugnacity irascible disdain distaste of the human condition aloof by income status unequaled in business perks gratuity compliments privilege that visualize massive American death tolls as tolerable curative. They see herd immunity as dark ages royalty viewed subjects sucking the royal treasury dry as obstacles to acquisition of wealth land power we are seen as expendable accidents ok to happen we are acceptable losses viewed more as cold stats than avid remarkable intelligent worthy persona able to achieve mastery over farcical chosen barrier erected barricade against Civilized modernity through Health and Safety.

I like to envision our human condition as avid remarkable intelligent worthy persona able to achieve mastery over a challenging environment adroit at using civilized minds to tame the harshest crisis sooth the savage beast that is America.

I have to admire almost pay homage to the destitute inane lack of repulsive antibodies societal not organic biological to act as efficiently as white blood cells in attacking neutralizing rendering harmful cellular societal viral germs benign. There's no such thing here acting as a positive non-corrosive shield against caustic informational onslaught chided tweaked over emphasized singular focus insular onerous deviant motivationally devious preconceived notions of Coup American Mass Murder using viral pandemic to kill Americans. Gleaning them for cash first of course now also seems this now coincides with a massive Russian cyber-attack on our institutions vulnerable by sustained attack 4-pandemic front. Russian strike takes into account Trumpdemic machination call for millions of Americans to be infected caught off guard we have become victims this attack is a war instigation mechanism Republican efforts may be more well planned than previously thought. They are on a mission to murder us pull the wool over our eyes take the wax out of your ears roll up your sleeves spit on your hands rub "em together and let's give these blighters a good swift kick in the pants! Quite!

And they're off coming out at the gate Pharmaceutical labs running now around the first turn fastest creation of an effective vaccine against pandemic doom in any century task well done now beating the turf vying for the center post rail shipping inter-state conglomerates railroad air cargo competing now neck and neck rounding the second turn far corner of the racetrack government institutions typically slow out of the starting gate are gaining halfway through the middle of the far turn they are now again pose to play they part professionally planning distribution of vaccinations throughout the land coming around the far turn they have lagged behind coming down the stretch labs have millions of doses in there warehouses not moving for a lack of communication and coordination shipping is dependent upon demand for destination at the finish line a photo finish the most hep adept all are inept. Tally Ho!! Mos Def!! Post timin' for dis rhymin!

We should have seen this coming Trumpdemic running interference for Russian operations since having Election help to victory refusing any statements or sanctions for Russian incursion using the pandemic as a smoke screen no commitment to action on public health and safety trouncing trade and the economy dissolution of alliances with benefactors criminal negligence in no pandemic response depletion of resistance resources limited voracious insatiable glutenous satiation dining on our American vulnerabilities now plagued by 4 pandemics Russia has had us under attack unobserved as Trumpdemic used media TV as the medium to obfuscate redirect attention from our National Security by centering himself as the object of our disgraceful obsession with celebrity while the message a Russian massage of our over confidence launching A Pearl Harbor Cyber Modern-Day Blitzkrieg heinous successful at knocking this country on its pompous haughty arrogant buttocks diminutive on its enormous fat behind. Something as obese as the US getting knocked down ain't going to get up quick this is for lack of a better term damn we're in a tight spot but it is clear now more than ever UNCLE SAM NEEDS YOU to be violated when our guard is down is treacherous vile despicable defecation on all of us our mandate forward from now on must reflect obsequious endeavors to incorporate more anticipatory defense strategies to augment goals to preserve our freedoms privacy sanctity of our shores sanctuary shelters of our homes to quote Youngsters "Rig the Rhymes, Get Ready to go to War" 'cause we need to Grab Our Bats to beat down Russia's front Door.

How many ways can this administration seek to condemn deprive the ill-fated depraved stealing everything in sight our Democracy Patriotism Health and Safety Decency Image Respect Expectations Tolerance Rationale Reason Integrity Honor Courage Respect for Knowledge Scientific Achievement Humility Reticence Trust Grace Sacrifice Dedication as devious as Trumpdemic family traits exhale exude the muck of skullduggery chicanery using government institutions as a method of strongarming. Burning our buildings scare tactic to now take backdoor behind-the-scenes covert control of millions of vaccine doses in multiple warehouses 'cross the country either selling it to the highest bidder. Us here in harm's way endangered or someone somewhere else in the world willing to shell out big time for life-saving remedy that should be free to all. You would have thought for the past few years you have seen every horror in

American schema now craven dastardly cowardice seditious. Now to propagate seek to earn blood money selling vaccine at ever increasing prices as the demand increases as shipments become mishandled if there was ever a time for a Superhero now would be a good time don't want to rush you but things are getting pretty dicey here right about now almost don't know which way to turn stuck between a rock and a hard place damned if you do damned if you don't I'd like to say I've had just about enough to Trumpdemic menaces now go on now git you all and the drama that is they mamma.

Where are the heroes when you need them? Are we really just now aware of the Russian preemptive nefarious notorious instigative infamous 1st Strike of World War III? Trumpdemic machinations has roughed us up just enough to soften us up relaxed our grip on reality related to National Defense caught us off guard with our pants down snogging the hired help distracted tending to a miss in the Rolls-Royce engine warm up torn whether to drive it or the Ferrari to get fast food or hit the ho stro even Maestros too preoccupied with petty opulence stupefied senses dulled to even mount natural defense mechanisms as Russia now prepares to plow us under as a matter of routine anticipating no opposition to stealthy insurrectionist occupation and take over they were the underdogs in their trade and economic development lending to stagnation now about to topple the Sleeping Giant. Shame on us for this letting it get to this point in our Cosmic Calendar Journey talk about dropping the ball no choice but to get back in the game play to win 'cause we got to knock this one out the ballpark to quote an indelible phrase: "He hit a long ball, it's a way out there annnnd gone," at this time we need to bring The BABE outta death extended retirement have him pinch hit and point to the field when he takes his turn at bat where he will place the home run that or Willy Mays putting another one outta the ballpark brings back our confidence in our pastime nationalism renewed passion to take pride once again proud to be American.

Here Yee! Here Yee! Here Yee! Now let it be known machinations throughout the land and the world beyond that his prostate Trumpdemic the flatulent Him he who allowed it to flourish has scribed his will on parchment Twitter that the masses beware of the free press and of professional government Intelligence gathering (unequaled on earth), but to pay heed homage to his royal babble rabble his brothers in Mother Russia had nothing to do with this facial slapping they after all they really had just defecated on all of us his hiney suggests we should bestow our lives to toil over China as the preferred objective of our shyly displayed inattention feigned condemnation as his royal hiney's rotundos derriere blasts past gas to expose to noxious foul odor permeating every corner of the Planet Earth in others words Trumpdemic the flatulent had made this whole place smell like ASS! Every picture tells a story, don't it?

Okay, let's for just a minute or two discuss the world of Mainstream very important to us all yet in a recent parchment barf Trumpdemic equates as Lamestream going now into processing what's really going on fringe the cusp jagged edge splintered cuttings outskirts outlying regions shady areas discreet intangible jaded slippery slope metered descent into unscrupulous vain indecency villainous attrition erudite atrocious off centered out of bounds just out of alignment this describes the machinations Trumpdemic and cohorts should be held accountable for criminal traitorous conspiracy being just plain odd is no excuse.

Are my eyes misleading? Have we not now been confirmed in a First Strike Russian attack aided by Trumpdemic machination centering our attentions on celebrity voracious hoarding not on National Defense Trumpdemic has been the decoy all along when all is done his insane traitorous anathematic persona will get paid to sell us out all of us. The realization our Freedoms are being ceompromised for individual gain. This is one of the most heinous historical examples of Benedict Arnold plotting demise. Used to be they hit us we hit back. 4 major pandemics have crippled our resolve Trumpdemic and Russia used and abused us sabotage impending ruination looming we cannot be half assed about this time to act let's get started take this nation out of the dark with trash removal.

Something is better than nothing. The COVID-19 Stimulus Relief Bill is happening way slow almost too little too late the miserly societally visible machination result of perverted proselytic proclivitous personalities in gatekeeper positions of legislative power control of repression tactics using deprivation measured minimal gratituitive handouts to keep an underclass incognito disguised as poor and maintain a labor class of working dependent middle-class girdled harnessed using bridal and blinders to steer direction stingy cutting Individual relief and nipping back Unemployment Benefits because the damage is done and continuing this will not make up for already endured losses suffering 24/7. Hell enough is enough why does it seem like we are sheep being herded why is no one saying what really should be uttered we are facing dire emergency threat disguised as tech intrusive change the nuclear codes the moment you can wrestle it from his megalomaniacal hands prepare for scenarios atypical unanticipated real consequences of Trumpdemic pandemic dilemma cannot provide impetus for Russian overthrow of the US. What next mutated COVID-19 virus? As a matter of fact yes seeing now a Variant reported from UK, South Africa, Belgium, Germany what about China no reporting of variant really something is afoot now the 4-pandemic threat has kicked it up a notch 5-pandemic enigmatic anomaly rampaging human domain acting now like a Smart Virus anticipating our responses attempting to outmaneuver our every effort this is now a miscarriage waiting to be a calamity inside a royal disaster that would screw up a wet dream now you don't have to look hard to see to know what's really going on. We are knee deep in it (ok to substitute another four-letter word).

If the shoe fits the most recent machinations Trumpdemic barf Twitter parchment says all you need to know about the fifth regimen Nazi in disguise everything about Him he who allowed it to flourish points to him working like Heinrich Himmler to do a hastily practiced shabby Hitler impersonation nothing else explains the enigma that is Trumpdemic the flatulent Him he who allowed it to flourish more precisely than Nazi in disguise to do the Russian bidding to sell us all out to first enamor American TV fanaticism use it and taxation manipulation for intent to cheat the gov. for personal gain stealing billions in redirecting wealth and from gov. budgets emollients ingratiation deficit increase destruction of trade economy deprivation to build poverty intolerance acceptance of inappropriate extremism attack on Lamestream bureaucracies murderous withholding of information and medical response readiness purposeful interference with life-saving measures on a federal scale causing desperate dog-eat-dog bidding states competing for fed aid. Tthere is no end to what a Nazi in the presidency can and will do, ladies and gentlemen, there is LEVEL 7 Eminent Threat go to DEF CON now infiltrator is planning more with help from others like shamed Gen Flynn Ret. Felon Confessed Liar pardoned lots of turkeys not fit for consumption pooping up the roost time to change the newspaper in the bottom of the cage shame on us for being deceived by these rooster pooh motherfuckers though I know Trumpdemic had a good hiding place America a land where this intrepid menace could breed freely unobstructed among white supremacists able to wield wealth as social armor built by the gods don't know about you I'm not willing to turn the other cheek if it walls like a duck quacks like a duck when in a process of elimination avenues are exhausted whatever remains must be pertinent Trumpdemic federal flow has painted us into a corner now let's fire his unscrupulous incompetent Nazi ass because the curtain will close on this bad act and then Overture this is it tonight's the night here it is we'll hit the heights and oh what heights we'll hit on with the show this is it.

I got a bone to pick I don't want that Mitch McConnell monkey mouth motherfucker boffin mothers on my thrown again I'm mad but I ain't stressin' I'm mad got one question Mitch McConnell where were you when I was walking 'now you got the whole world talking King Totesmoker everybody wants to cut me up something kunta when you got the gams you got the power dat be to take it to the streets Mitch McConnell's whack thankin' stealin' all our money don't see much more need to render him wanna be dead and stinkin'.

We have nothing to fear but fear itself in this machination on our nation Trumpdemic the flatulent Him he who allowed it to flourish is not someone to be feared after all he is a rotund obese coward orange-white sveinhund with nasty yellow follicle damage clinging to his carcass that smells of ass death and decay fear is inappropriate he cannot see below his belly to determine if he is male or female revealing the contents of closet has outed his deceitful now using every deception to smash and grab he wants to be the center of the Universe but he forgot to put it in reverse we're besmirched good grief this place is the stressin delicatessen make a nigga want to break out the Smith and Wesson we know what to expect after four years of this queer we got nothin to fear the end of Trumpdemic is very near almost here.

The Christmas Star Jupiter and Saturn in alignment for us all to see presents the opportune moment to extend Seasons Greetings to everyone. Cherish health safety survival we Party next year.

This is a Dark ages moment the realization 2020 is the deadliest year on earth history and climbing. The chronic chaos our Educational system has been thrown into interrupting forward progress shutdowns clouding scholarships sports graduations post-graduate upward strides inhibited put on hold the psychological is messing with all of our minds once again we have as adults dropped the baton here we go again neglecting our children youth and young adults pandemic or not we are not providing the sanctuary needed to cultivate safe achievable futures for our path steers us through the mine fields of shattered America once an avenue of promise now mostly detrimental to our health hopes dreams.

If you want to see White Privilege up close feast your eyes on the misfit stooge defecating on anything everything everyone all over the world not even bothering to step outside the People's House. You all know all the foul mess subterranean blemish belching forth the spew out his Lame Duck bottom impact so widespread we all have to wear masks to not die of COVID-19 and prevent Trumpdemic duck butt spew from entering our mouths. With so many of these Mallard brained bereft retarded somehow consistently chosen as gatekeepers of normalcy power acceptance opportunity leadership wealth fame tolerance understanding boundaries constraints success failure condemnation admiration administration bureaucracies officers incarceration retaliation rehabilitation conciliation resignation aberrations generations of our lives thwarted. As if we should be backhanded for breathing the same air dreaming the same except not perverted futures especially not created by the quack whack ass freaks that claim all as mine mine mine mine mine one more time pardoning every criminal tom dick and harry might get you brownie points in your sissy like good ole white bread clubs throughout the land but from where I stand I stay out the way of you who crap their own dinner bowl.

So I've been a thinkin' it's about time to do somethin' about time and how it can help manage our successful futures man has since the Stone Age been trying to tame his environment bumbling through effort after imperfect effort using anything found on the ground in trees underground in caves underwater or whatever falls outta the sky. We continue to strive for human perfection Trumpdemic should be the slap in the face the wakeup call we have not been anywhere near redeeming now our time lives are slip sliding away we need to take control mastery of time improves potentials for timely viability. Time can be altered large stars and planets bend spacetime fabric of gravity. This flexing causes smaller objects to orbit the larger tilting or not in the revolution around time here increases and decreases now imagine there is a lot of this kind of planetary space bending twisting and flexing some of which can take the shape of funnel-like paths extending light years without reshaping unless collisions black holes are reinforcing some swallowing others these funnel-like paths are wormholes existent due to generated gravity can be focused to a singularity where time stands still at that moment a gravimetric frequency variable interaction modulation can put a Quantum ship in extra linear or cause you to transmigrate from linear to nonlinear time adjacent to our time but not influenced by our time. At this moment you have crossed boundaries and thresholds now Quantum navigating in another time and space thus you have achieved time travel for every micro-minisecond of your movement could place you at the Big Bang or 300 years into an uninhabited future this would take instrument calibrations. When we have gained Metacognition of time we can improve our human condition through quality time, time spent with friends, time with family, time for recreation, time for self-improvement, time for this time for that time to get hit with a wiffle ball bat hey what time is it really What Time is It?

Sorry about the duality, I was trapped in time appropriate timely!

If you have traveled through time how to prove it to someone is unclear. Besides the old watch comparison trick used in everyone's favorite *Back to the Future* trilogy here's something that I think would be very convincing present multiple versions of yourself instantly simultaneously able to make verbal and physical communicative overture gestures a modern day version of the mythical Hydra attention getting remarkable maybe a bit scary humbling to say the very least bequeathed behest to strive to be best of the best to create time of All the Rest.

Another conceivable way to crack the time barrier obstacle to futurism is to in a vacuum open multiple parallel singularities where there combined atomic force is overlapping at its greatest intensity produce a gravimetric vortex spiral a funnel-like gravity well a particle dropped into this well could eventually be a vortex navigable transport transmigration vehicle to accommodate time era exchange for humans.

The distance travelled into the spiral vortex will require years of monitored calibration to sight particular time destinations. More than 2 ways to skin a cat.

The American tragedy machinations at the Southern border thousands separated locked in crudely constructed animal cages subjected to terrible forms of confinement imprisonment chronic abuse over 600 children still not reunited with parents even though a standing Court order to do so, now we embrace the horror of American children orphaned having lost 1 or 2 parents to pandemic or Trumpdemic the two are synced. Families already strapped are torn to pieces as White Privilege flaunts itself like a parading rooster crowing at the crack whack pact of extremes the onslaught of acceptance of grotesque criminalism contrary to any normalcy. The fact that our government is this fatigued corrupted deluded harmful to most Americans who embrace the value to never assume the path observed by traitorous scumbags bent on selling us out for personal gain. We are not just pawns to be used on your play board oh and don't think that a very skilled Intelligent group of dedicated patriots couldn't engineer strategies to bring Trumpdemic mongers to poetic justice. Stripping there blood money fortunes invoking use of bug spray to get the roaches as they try to escape something can be done as they are not to bright would be easily bested as they are brainless freaks preoccupied with handing out human suffering. With that crowd of wealthy scum there isn't safety in numbers for they would turn on and eat each other a word to the vile Karma is a Bitch!

It must be agonizingly humiliating to be the right kind of white now in the face of wealthy powerful White Privilege machination ruthlessly driving into buildings smash and grab pillaging of everything of value in America our Judicial System National Treasury National Defense Security Agencies Legislative Bureaucracies Taxation Tarnation literally scraping out vital physiology from the backs of our eyeballs. If this sounds familiar to U.S. Military clandestine or not it was wrong. Check national treasures before the Russian Beverly Hillbillies Boris and Natasha Badinoff vacate the premises they want it for trinket shelf dust collection occupation now to be able to mercifully say begone but after the new Administration occupies the tainted mansion I assure you fumigation will not be enough. They will aspire to braggadocios boastfully claiming ascension to godlike status as a result of their extensive efforts to cause our pain there is a slight chance here as heinous becomes promiscuously abundant we may I hope witness episodes of them turning on each other a shark feeding frenzy indicative of the kind of dogs they are let's keep our fingers crossed.

Fate may have just bitten all of us right on the ass the HIV/AIDS virus that attacked humans.

Here as we procreate and recreate engineered as a smart virus to attack certain key genetics.

Efforts to enable efficient genocide released in poorest regions of Africa to promote spread.

Resultant worldwide implications infectious appocaustropic. The Flu virus death tolls up yearly.

Recently in China a news report of Super Soldiers could tie directly into flu mutation escape.

A deadly COVID-19 as genetic experimentation is the norm in China and control of all

Super Soldiers, however dark nefarious sinister ulterior motives is vicious not justifiable.

By any human measure. They have taken advantage of us all still they have us at a disadvantage.

Oh well! This is a fine mess you have gotten us into, Stanley! Aww Gee Willockers!

Smoothing out the sheer. Nothing like bringing in the sheeves or a rocking pneumonia burning down the house I'm trying to warn ya travel in a spiraling vortex gravimetric forces bending particles wavelengths quantum energy matter ionized radicalized universe a descent between surrounding parallel singularities the concentration of enough balance of forces to control the sheer in the gravity well incorporating safe regulated calibrated rate of fall and safely weathering external pressures being able to generate this in a confined space at reusable convenience will chart our future stairway to the stars Ad Infinitum to Infinity and Beyond.

When seeking a path to one's future you steer through many obstacles first and foremost you have to survive the formidable rearing the upbringing of which unfortunately some do not survive. I don't just mean death lack of survival in this circumstance can be sordid and you thought escaping the birth canal would do the trick seeking truth love education compassion friends companionship comfort making choices seeking safety at times sanctuary. There were two canyons that played into paved a path parallel to my own Laurel and Malibu music lifestyles from these areas seemed gainful abundant graceful charming. Alluring as it set a standard of tolerance achievement beauty luxury affordable not necessarily extravagance a memory of a time when hope health happiness seemed of primary import social bonding energized. We were impressed by the "All are fat and none are thin" of the Canyon Ladies pouring music down the canyons or "Come on baby light my fire, Love me two times girl," Doors opening doors a better day even as the spectre of Vietnam provided the impetus for the altered states now seen.

As the Trumpdemic machinations proclivitous proselytic murderous personalities sucking the life from us all white taking a dump defecating on America and Americans cancerous spreading destroying everything in its path we toil on bravely yet without certainty that now more than ever gov. does not have our backs. We are on our own every man for himself not acceptable our worth demands exoneration this vile in your face example of rampant White Privilege thievery lawlessness fiendishness lame incompetence cannot continue into our American futures. Elimination of undisciplined privilege in favor of rule of law balanced by truth justice not power and cronyism throw the Electoral College out with the bath water bring back People's Popular Vote. Set a course for a better possible future although the Canyons aren't quite as attractive now due to time progress scandal as Carol King put it in terms of positive energy still inspired to motivate us. Things we can see we can feel to change as passengers on the most successful spaceship earth "I feel the earth move under my feet."

Our ill-fated relationship with the enigma of coincidence being in the wrong place what can happen will in the matter of human time traversing we will need ways to for lack of scientific specific nomenclature to dial ourselves in. For it is possible that as we make strides towards the inevitable you may if choosing random destinations arrive at your own time of birth or death. Note not necessarily threatened by the encounter we've already been engaged in the type of information gathering that can help dial us in. Specific time frames worldwide documentation of everything from time of sunrise and sunset barometric pressure wind velocity sea level solar radiation cow poop methane by quantity of human excrement Hyperion plant. Now with the ice core samples of recorded earth days these samplings of atmospheric records daily can set up a schema for calculating present past and projected futures based on algorithm based calculations using present day data augmented by reasoned judgment.

Fighting 5 pandemics is apocastrophy nobody wanted it now brings us to the brink of realization our social infancy our never-ending continuing struggles to present reason as an alternative to racist racial bias at a time when the Front Line Hospital lifesavers are of mixed ethnic heritage all working to save lives a mega priority and yet instances of black medical personnel dedicated themselves become infected Medical Doctors are being treated differently because of their skin color until they have been formally tied to the hospital admittance registration ID. Doctors who put themselves in harm's way to care for the sick should be exalted for they are the heroes we see too little of. Uncalled for racial bias at a time of pandemic universal threat to all is monstrous sinister heathen irrational irascible nefarious heinous we need to Come Together Right Now to fix this shit we cannot stoop to act like the child like example set by our worst historical Executive Failure Trumpdemic the flatulent Him he who allowed it to flourish. United we stand Divided we fall we fail to cure, govern, fix our nation strive for remedy successful recovery abundance plentiful normalcy satiation we can arrive at a hopeful point in our future lives where and when we can say, "One and one and one are three got to be a joker 'cause he's so hard to see Come Together Right Now," so we can be

Free.

A wave-riding experience of any lifetime anywhere anyplace the possibility exists for excursions adventures into space and time locating places in a planetary abundant Universe or sampling time era exchange potentials. North shore Hawaii is home to Waimea 100-foot peaks contestants yearly surf this challenge at 68 years old quite a risk even if younger because of big predators I'll stick now to water skiing. In another scenario we find a 10,000-foot liquid oxygen methane or hydrogen wave in a large planetary ocean in a Smart Gel bodysuit and a Gel molecular adaptable board Bonsai last one to the bottom scuba water ski on Jupiter Ocean moon hang golden over Venus or we can just go birdwatching watch the big birds in the Jurassic period fun in the present past future is here for the taking doers seeking out to embrace redo the Great Awakening.

Sacrifice suffering facing reality things no attentive coping person can avoid in this time of shared nightmarish extremes. More isolation than ever in modern memory missed opportunities dashed hopes dreams goals chosen paths futures more destitute than not though vaccine promises outcomes still not perfect unpredictable in scope stifling lives. Respect to those businesses that were ruined closed entrepreneurs disabled many having losses troublesome to salvage your future is imperative but for now asking more of some citizens to absorb closure to survive till safe is akin to patriotism. It's hard for everyone but we all got to pitch in to win.

COVID-19 Stimulus Relief Bill finally signed at the last possible microsecond after bipartisanship hacks out an agreement bordering brinkmanship again and again seen consistently throughout our legislative history a practice seen as neglectful cumbersome as machination rich control of political systems rears its ugly head now we know to be tainted stained Russian influences leaving a visible mark traitorous acculturated as norm yet continuing in our faces to use deceit treachery disdain distaste for passing bills that demonstrate a necessity to provide economic support due to societal obstacles to upward mobility economic cultural to majority people of color degreed or not. This tendency to go beyond the brink is the best example of machination   biased prejudiced proclivitous perverted proselytic murderous personalities reluctant to share wealth thus in this country prosperity for most cannot exist a damn shame because after all we fought for everything we go through prosperity here is overdo also right for me and you.

Haters, I'm singing to you this is what I got what I have to do how do I know how come 'cause it's where I came from can't you see it now I thought I did it the right way I tried to get to rich working hard I had to stop at I had money In the bank but nuttin' in my pocket I learned my lesson from a slick hooker bitch and a cab driver itching fast fussin' you give it to the company boy boy boy you out here for yoself hustlin' gots to be strapped locked cocked with a phat knot this how to show what you got. Nihea I'm tired a you all up in the club actin sick illin' see like you got yo shit down easily when most of youuu come up broken thugs only yo Mamas could love ya now this nigga drop down on you like the heavens above till all you mothers be hollering give us some love gots to be strapped locked cocked with a phat knot Hater or not. (Lay down the beats here)

The massive task of American Life saving vaccinations moving across the country state to state using prioritized methods deemed necessary to prudent is more formidable than Ali Liston or Leonard Hearns needing to reach over 335,000000 people is daunting at 10,000000 every 5 days it could take 5-6 mos. in truth you know that is not a reasonable goal it's as stupid as Operation Warp Speed 20,000000 by year's end yeah right not going to be. It may take literally 1-2 years 85 percent vaccinated then perhaps herd immunity long-term solutions are inescapable due to the slash and burn tactics of dubious traitors crippling recovery. Using Fed work projects more important than ever starting with intelligent use of modern technology and thinking to solve multiple problems using sustainability as model for solutions. For example our nation suffers drought in the west water rich snow rich in the Midwest southeast northeast and East Coast building a Water Reclamation Storage Sewage Separation Purification Plant Facility built starting in New Orleans and Mississippi below sea level using a system that collects all water run off including sidewalk street melting grids melt and funnel snow plow expanding this system to each state across the nation employment to accomplish goals having the old system collapse engineering design features into the new target put country back to work. Bring water to West Coast one hundred percent improvement of water management our most vital resource typically wasted squandered and finally a realization of clear and straight thinking.

The good things about this Water Reclamation Storage Sewage Separation Purification Plant Facility conform to the urgency presented by imminent 5-pandemic enigma jumpstarting economy. Employing massive state to state hiring process work force training implementation of skills level training in salary recognition community recoveries gradual rebuilding of operational business franchise store fronts promenades mall entertainment venues Federal funds directed to sensible construction to enhance our Nation. No wasting time manpower money to build stupid walls separating us from our southern neighbors which I see as counterproductive. Extending the Plant Facility South of the Border Down Mexico Way we could kill 2 birds with 1 stone International Contracts mutually beneficial and get down to really Play with clean drinking Water tequila shots all the day South of the Border Down Mexico Way. I don't know about you all but I'm a missin' the flava on a mission to savor flava of Siesta de Cabo De San Lucas. Now you know I gots to have it I got more to say proven by months of verbosity but somebody has got to say something speak truth to power of restraint. It should be obvious just look around things are really broken here aren't working right shit ain't happening a fix involves selfless real motives. One area is unskilled labor a majority in many parts of the country in each case barring age or medical background put them to work provide the promise once again of for a grateful nation one-day stories may be told of the Shovel Men of Appalachia beating crew times of wealthy machined crews in the North. Point is hope through salary supporting family structures honing in with pinpoint accuracy on How to Fix a Nation Post Trumpdemic Machinations 2020-21.

The President elect and Vice President elect have now both been vaccinated Mrs. Harris took it in stride not like the babbling pussy Sen. Rubio who spoke of his pale appearance and looked away closed his eyes to get the shot. Only 6 cases reported of allergic reactions in 2,000,000 hopefully no long-term side-effects like male or female sterility will show but think of a shutdown continuing for months into 2021 then a governor back to work order is met with massive lack of availability of employment hiring opportunities Federal work programs should be a necessary vital part of supplying job lifelines now what improvements can be made to fix old existing conditions that inhibit limit our lives take the Canadian example and clean up neighborhoods throughout each city changing the ugly appearances of dilapidated communities providing social cultural relief we clean up our act. It has been needed same with government processes close options for the heinous White Privilege good ole orange-white Russian criminals showing out while laughing at us expose this behavior as intolerable have news agencies stop feeding the racist fascists supremist dissident madness ban Channel 11 broadcast as White Nationalism insurrectionism expose Facebook and Twitter nuts ban extremist posts renew patriotism ethics and values pride in service employment labor lifestyles make moves to improve lives because Trumpdemic has barfed on the world that's it no more don't dominate the whack jack let's get our mack back.

I've had lots of jobs with the usual mix of satisfaction and grief eventually nailing a salary almost commensurate with skills not capabilities I turned down a sales position with an auto parts conglomerate I was enticed to take that position at a martini lunch where a scantily clad most attractive young white woman danced to the music of Cabaret on our table as we dined it is the closest I have come to a position of employment that offered a three 3 I repeat 3 martini lunch it is now apparent why this shit don't work professional politicians are alcoholics drinking before they make vital decisions if some of these white boys they mostly white or anything like some I had to cover for who could not hold they liquor it makes sense so much crap is hitting the fan you can almost hear the burps or is it belches. Whatever. Breathalyzer, please. Whew!!

I awoke today to look at the disgraceful conduct of our government and criminal justice processes prisoners across the nation 2-4 times more likely for infection no plans to include prisons in vaccinations then the corrupt consistency of police officers once again no Federal charges in the Tamar Rice murder by police. I find this particularly disturbing for if you watched the video of this heinous act clearly a white cop shot a child in his face damn the thought that gave birth to their foul stench-ridden rotten asses in addition COVID-19 vaccinations may extend into years if we don't step up the pace also a new legislator elect just passed due to COVID-19 41 years old our days are filled with morbid grotesque harsh life-threatening trauma we carry on expecting positive gains but are stepped on trounced pummeled by nuts Russian flavor sordid incompetence as if they are willing to use these present circumstances as an opportunistic culling event killing off those undesirable. As most have survived this Christmas without even crumbs to give to Tiny Tim as homelessness hunger starvation pick off family after family Moscow Mitch still plays his favorite game Russian roulette with for our lives in this moment of reflection could there not have been another way instead of the current now inescapable in lethality. Yes, there was but greed power wealth posed the existential corruption now dominating our tentative futures. Bravo to all the creeps out there caused this Bravo you indiscreet murderous assassins way to go you fucking nuts.

Irony the elusive lingering after effect of occurrence anticipated or not impacting the victims and event history. *Twilight Zone* Rod Serling in an episode depicted endless searing Sunlight increasing temperatures that melted an oil painting in a New York apt. seems a woman was dreaming feverish when she awoke scenario was in reverse her their reality was earth becoming a frozen planet in endless darkness. Here our reality is raging burning viral contagion simultaneously Global warming hotter temperatures rising sea levels the future of which then becomes a frozen planet planetary snow ball perception or misfortune of galactic fate which forecasted this in satire. A turmoil approaching as climactic as two black holes colliding nowhere to run nowhere to hide we're being funneled into a flow pattern that holds intrinsic influence pertinent to moving forward yet giving way to skepticism depending on successes regulated by authority currently caustic corrosive clandestine corrupted corroded by years of pandering to competence by nihilistic neglect resultant implication of ruling class arid complacency in other words "Of thee I see."

Happy New Year, be safe and warm.

First day of the New Year U.S. death tolls record high 20,000,000 Iran wants to use opportunity provided by this no leadership moment in time to wage war Trumpdemic still trying to appeal to whimsical fairies to turn Election results stimulus checks for some which should have been like government handshakes more a mosquito bite vaccinations way to slow body counts piling mortuaries can't keep pace Surgeon General's wife infected we are now so victimized by our tendencies in nihilism neglectful adherence to cumbersome arid complacency waiting until the last minute to repel assault instead of proactive mediating incendiary response targeted focused solutions executed with precise logistics curative effect outcomes generated we cannot wait anymore. No time to lose can't pull up stakes and disappear timing is everything no slackers stop dragging feet people are lying crying dying Trumpdemic ringing in 2021 with a political spectacle stunt machinations shameful in the wake of this morbidity but typical to their prejudices with all our lives now caught up in mass inappropriate movements drag us all along we are not yet again seeing dead in the streets such as after Katrina but they're already in trailers in many places and mounting soon we may have to cover the deceased as we go back to whatever jobs still may exist make no mistake this is a wakeup call to arms action unrivaled by previous sought after accomplishments failure is not an option we gotta get this right reason why half of the whole world might die my my come on y'all in 2021, I believe we can.

Ok, I'm sick of it all this following a lame duck running around like grandpa running 'round the house with a smelly loaded diaper plans for January 5 delay Senate confirmation a bad movie but we can't change the channel it's on every one you would think as impatient as rich redundant mental deficients are they would tire of this baby babbling I thought NASA was stuck on stupid glad to know Biden Harris cannot be more of same for I am assured they can walk and chew gum at the same time and both tie their own shoes. Amen.

Make a list take notes make a schematic representation of the names of the oligarchs in Senate on Tuesday that will make a visible public attempt to overthrow the will of the people have their names districts representative committee designations photos on signs post them everywhere they are willing to crap on Democracy rejecting people of color as participants or human beings deserving Liberty. Talk about lock them up we need to keep these cusses where we can see them at all times people like that really bother me.

Almost hard to believe what is seen and heard Trumpdemic

machinations pursuant to a criminal madman not to be confused with the hit TV drama the actions taken to sway push bribe corrupt Election officials to taint results tilt or turn or twist reality to favor diabolical maniacal ends is more than just surreptitious it's grotesque self-power gorging uncontrolled rampant rampaging megalomania. He needs Clinical help he is a danger to himself and others he needs medical personnel to respond to an immediate recoup overwhelming intensive psychological treatment for detractive neurological brain disfunction locked away for years of treatment to comprehend his level of enjoyment of destruction of America its Democratic character its institutions its citizens. Armed still with Moscow Mitch dangling 2000 over the heads of the people to see how high we can leap for it to encourage us to see them as savior I already pay my taxes yearly I'm kissing too much ass as it is. This bitch ass Trumpdemic has been down and dirty out the gate as practiced as U.S. at Interventions globally literally having authored volumes of the most dirty. Does it seem peculiar that Trumpdemic this creep is an issue? Does to me even nihilistic neglect and resultant arid dismissive complacency is not a catalyst for current visible extremes in mental redundancy thus ulterior motives drive the current national discourse infantile subliminal vain seditious insurrectionist speaking recruitment of similar insanity to deny the will of the American people. I've had all I can stand and I can't stand no more somebody break out the large can of spinach eat the whole damn thing and get busy like Popeye kicking ass quake beat down this fake.

I've been around for a while I've endured the usual ton of crap sails into your path I've bolstered my character against assaults earthly physical esoteric intrepid valuing my contribution to the Universe I have to say I am humbled by the impact of the spectacle of Trumpdemic machinations unchained white narcissistic vanity squandering or time in our lives actually killing in the hundreds of thousands must have on decent white folks because we know they are out there what is troubling to me has to be a lot for those of normative decency to have to witness shame on Trumpdemic shame on you.

People throughout my life would not be withholding stark commentary about the moraceous inane vomit projectile to quote a popular movie streaming from the mouths of Trumpdemic

Republicans' butts spouting flames out they mouths like a butane lighter the stench in our nation is toxic noxious tepid appallamendous odorous stale dead and stankin' in the air in our clothes houses on our skin in our hair in our noses in our mouths. Just like COVID-19 tryin' best to kill you we need to breathe independent oxygen supply to escape contamination cannot stop spread because people want it there is no other explanation dreary dark as it is we would not be infected like this unless a false sense of security exists on a large scale. Balance the equations sometimes you have to factor in others cancel out incorporating all multiple functions to arrive at a solution although most of us can't immediately accurately quote prime numbers out to 25 places many can and do better than that practice makes perfect Trumpdemic cautery be illin get on bitch bring back real chillin'. Y'all come back now!

Happy to renounce the atrocious concepts of suspended animation a medical induced sleep status to accomplish long space sojourner journeys not required in the Quantum ship as the mode and speed of travel bridges gaps in the relationship between aging and distance to destination. This stasis is dangerous as the occupants are helpless at the mercy of automated systems fallible unreliable useless in a practical sense perhaps in the future like traveling coach more affordable longer to get there. The Quantum ship offers us exceptional ways to observe our own history in most unique ways transports some of which already may have been seen by privileged few as UFO close encounters for it is reasonable to predict we would investigate ourselves. This may offer some semblance of relief about possible futures, however look at what's up now info about a tech advanced future without people of color has infiltrated seeped into the lure akin to deep state but the US Navy has firsthand proof of great concern to all non-white a result of the Phoenix experiment. WWII hell TV shows have had us seeing walking through walls since the 70s. We live in a world of light but we are kept in the dark treated as if we can't comprehend the tangible due to inclination to frivolous pursuits. Sadly a lack of access to sourcing materials to build for the future is the real prison here on earth denying goal accomplishments due to economic social retardation. Tragic the effect is wasted manpower heterogenaity human kinds greatest asset.

Republicans and Trumpdemic machinations proclivitous

enthusiasts are going through withdrawals the inevitable harsh attempts to regain a semblance of normative decency in Intelligence not currently observed ulterior motive for this behavior apparently stems from people of color especially their concepts of black community no longer worshipping the white master as God a far cry from the original colonizer encounter where indigenous black coastal tribal people tried to wash the first whites ever seen thinking skin color was painted. Never realizing it was really important for another reason the whites at that time were afraid of water did not bath the tribe was really doing itself a favor for I assure you the white colonizers stunk after a long sea crossing. l don't feel sorry for the creeps who have failed to launch but much like their smelly colonizer cousins can really stink up everything all this because they cannot except we no longer endure white man got a god complex now white complexities must get over it and themselves wake up grow up shout out to the masses we have outgrown crass no need for they asses.

I just got there sorry it took me so long the overwhelming detriment soiling our lives America our treasure our land of promise whitewashed beyond recognition tainted tarnished toppled candy ass rich sissies to prep pampered to be embarrassed humiliation seen clearly through their lying eyes orange-white Russian sweaty wrinkled frowns enabled by perverted aspersions resentment channeled by dismissive arid complacency arrogant in demeanor traitorous culpable delinquent fetish decaying minds wanting to contaminate all I thought it only went on in the 50s but this shit here is retro creepy this ain't hooked on Barbie this shit be all about "It's My Party"!

One just one good thing comes from the Trumpista's clown show the most white bunch of pale albino bleached blanched scoured scrubbed opaque pasty powdered painted pompous pussies got together in support of throwing out the white power Ace in the hole the Electoral College it would save a lot of time and thereby loads of money this is of govt. benefit a must for any keen charming intellectual dominion capable of inspirational visionary deeds and actions to strike forth carve forge a more direct less circuitous path to the promise land.

How haughty can you be looking down at us all from your perch oddly like that of Batman yielding your membership in club opulence flaunting your indecency woeful dereliction of duty rejecting sworn oath to the Constitution and the people. Happily watching disadvantaged die by the hundreds of thousands dragging us to the brink of whatever hell y'all primarily inhabit occupy ok with suffering you caused and continue to dispense befouled rhetoric chronic time consuming as if this is not enough you furthermore steal from and cost the system of government you work for to do the will of the people money the most scarce resource elusive to most by design the sickness associated with this is not benign.

The driving forces thrusting our futures with balanced drivetrains power gliding differentially dispersing us like vehicles on a massive conveyance thoroughfare subject to changes in flow patterns bottlenecked due to 5 pandemic epidemic our inchoate bold velocity now slowed impeded our courses recalculated daily mileage no longer meaningful just mounting desperation critical survival management fuel to sustain not propel to progressively upward mobility on hold indefinitely paused demurred delayed this itself is undeserved not palatable unpleasance in resignation of deluge emergencies demand commanding undivided attention rigid adherence to self-preservation. Double masks plexiglass social distancing no more super-spreader events sold out for God sakes let's deal with this evil place because we got to get more power to the people roll out.

I'm tired now but I think they are going to call it for Ossoff it might finally happen in our lifetime a Democratic administration with control of Congress and Senate reigning in the repressive Moscow Mitch reeling in the scourge of the Atlantic gutting him just like freshly hooked cod afishy Republicans from wafting lingering refusing to dissipate. If this comes to realization our lives could change actually positively but hold up wait a minute we still got the 5 pandemic enigmatic atrocious antagonistic everywhere you look destination vaccinations moving across the nation because this is about hard times a coming you better be sure these hard times will drive you door to door hard times coming you can be sure these hard times be harder than ever been before.

As we boldly embark travelers on the good ship promise we are entangled in the cloaked web of machinations deceit incessant unending encroachment dubious seditious actions bent on gobbling all power dismantling Americanism to install Russian nationalism as compatible elements of someone's traitorous Republicanism now focus of attention this is really the never-ending story years and years of drama you can keep it I've had a whole life of it and don't want to repeat the shit the burden weighing us down like an anchor and depleting every valuable already scarce resource weakening our ability to enact and complete repairs taxing everything costly time consuming. We cannot work fast enough to accomplish solutions as we are tethered to deathly futures looming with so much in this morbid mix is survival still possible or is the recovery threshold beyond our reach. At some point we may have to consider with all the turmoil we have lost sight of sensibility and may ultimately be victims of nihilistic neglect acceptance of corroded societal remains.

The money pit bottomless never-ending supplies stashing of cash stockpiles gold reserves foundations of national treasures backbones of economies able to develop using domestic and international foreign exchange markets possessed in abundance by relative few. Meaning of life and death for most I am appalled by the antics machinations of wealthy exhibitionist politicians needlessly wasteful over indulgence in stalling legislative processes using the guise of debate to stymie waste valuable time all the while burning dollars in raging inferno of rhetorical deception facade lunacy barbarism sleight of hand a hearty shell game determination of the winners inherent lending restrictions to those able to dip into the abyss of wealth of a nation continues to be disturbing. The Real Politik seen often enough to have outgrown frustration now just evidence of sustained sociocultural abuse. Driving the wrong way into moving traffic hurling us toward collision with stark truth inundating us daily short cuts to success are encouraged by 5 pandemic enigma necessitating effective yet economical remedies national treasuries are not inexhaustible the hogs to our system need to be separated out some for slaughter giving way to cultural mercy.

Not my idea of the best use of my tax dollars, boy, these "It's My Party, I'll Cry if I Want To" guys none of which probably pays income tax are ruining even mighty white impudence impugning publicly unashamed for the cost to those of us who pay the cost to be the boss.

The price of Republican crybaby shenanigans to is a price too high to pay today's rage against the machine inspired by Trumpdemic speech to trash Washington, D.C., has cost a woman a valuable human being her life shot in cold blood truth already being covered up renegade stampede for sale the world to see how sadly morose juvenile perversion is deadly. Now you've gone and done it take all the credit you want for this one the disaster of failed treason you Trumpdemic proclivitous perverted proselytic murderous anal asinine assout asswrecked ass backwards droll assholes.

There should be no end to the public outcry of the machination attack on our government today placing fear into the hearts and minds of tolerant patriots women and children people endangered by people over conflicted jealousy unleashed for no good purpose. I never wanted to see or be taught this I would prefer to forget but worthwhile people died a fatal attraction to mass hysteria and it will be used to teach tolerance. Unfortunately bringing it into view ugliness undesirable miserable disgusting dysfunctional could you set no worse example of irrational irresponsibility mob mentality white people not afraid of police had it been black people many would be dead. Double standard two-tiered representation executive privilege extending to wealthy and powerful who opted to occupy expend our time in the most stupidly extravagant frivolous manner. You have no shame hard to be proud to be an American today.

The tragedy of insurrectionist mass hysteria yesterday in which all participants should be prosecuted to the fullest extent of the law we know shit has been broken here for years we have resigned ourselves to use contempt grief as daily burden of failed culture to the ugly societal feature of the Good Ole Boys club patronized exclusively by filthy rich opulence for centuries who care only of themselves and deny access to civilized. Yesterday shows there are a lot of these mob mentality brutes mentally deficients need for crisis counseling apparent not getting the help they need tearing everything down in their rage without help morbidity rates already up now explosive since nuts like this may not seek help but only aspire to destroy. Viable creative solutions are mandate we have just butted heads with unchecked widespread ignorance not surprising we knew it was here bewildering some 60-80 million people in this nation who endorse return to slavery not just black all people of color and complex docile religions serving a value in communities non-white despite income disparitie. To clean up this mess is a doting challenge for even God having to live so close to this kind of vile is suspect. Was it always the plan to place good citizens in Good Ole Boy sights so they could target us mercilessly? I don't enjoy the flava of the bad taste in my mouth left by antics of people who hate unresponsive to a shared Liberty. If no one can encourage maturity to battle this infantile childishness can we at least develop anti-racist pacifiers to keep them subdued from more drama a timeout for these fugitives from rug rats is insufficient.

One of the shady areas I have to fathom from the agreed disappointment on January 6 fringe things that find their way into only shades of grey the police force guarding the Nation's Capital Senate Congressional Leaders inept to the extent witnessed really! Is this just another example of complacency status quo broken institutions temporarily shored up against the next barrage of crooked entourage legislators paid off to placate not irradicate extremes or something else more sinister subtle damning was it a ploy rouse deceitful plot by multiple agencies police city state to bring more funds to policing a irrefutable appeal to the public law enforcement under duress the very killers marauding throughout our cities murdering the helpless innocents sad to think this but these institutions are plagued by legislative machinations inadequacies presenting economic impacts which may compel this clandestine farce into action starting with identification of seditious participants. You who started and perpetuate our decline I think you better recognize who you are dealing with son because one way or another this darkness got to give.

The damage is done. It's been a long hard fight continuing to chase the elusive goal Freedom Liberty Justice Promise Land Hope Dreams Happiness Prosperity under attack machination for generations increasing now in intensity forcing massive defensive postering to hold the lines of defense patriotism morals values on the line overrun now collapsed alarms sounded emergency sirens blazing while our long shot the American experiment goes down in flames panic is now a part of daily life the attacks not coming from outside enemy but the dark opposite this enemy has come from within sparked by centuries of cultivated hate now when we are at our weakest this culture to acculturate racial supremism more destruction chaotic skirmishes detrimental look at what we had what we have and what we've got we have to fight for life love happiness hopes dreams right to worship and recreate we cannot wait outcomes will depend on how we fought for we may still be here tomorrow but your dreams may not.

Actions of the last several months have clearly demonstrated machination the impact of inciteful rhetoric divisive seditious insurrectionists speaking at large planetary super-spreader gatherings which can instantly become a mobile armed strike force with insular single minded target Representative Democracy lifeblood covariant of the dream. Freedom and Liberty temporarily on hold calm for now but pensive national tension so thick you can cut it with a knife held back by threat of turning tide stockpiling privilege arrogance haughtiness prejudices extremisms weapons blood money grift proceeds to be used for the final assault. For you see we have just shown revealed abhorrently to a madman the power of destruction through modeling hatred he is now primed like a pedigree with a hard on with one more twist of the crank this dickwad will crack more unleashing apocastrophy. We have no time to waste every available moment prepare for onslaught for the scenario is foreboding the jig is up we can and will do better we know now what to expect. You can light the path to paradise and freedom but cannot force recalcitrants to use it let us not be fooled or surprised again by human redundancies incapable of wiping their own butts.

What is the healing process talked about when Biden takes over on the 20th of January? Is it just the shameful thuggish U.S. seen on Tuesday or the atrocious abuse abandonment of Democracy of the past 4 years? Are we talking cultural healing from police murder of black people nationwide or the suffering dying of white leadership failed response to threatening pandemic crisis? Can it be perceived healing has to come about from incessantly failed legislative management bureaucratic inefficiency judicial prejudices economic disparity intolerances there are so many issues and areas that need fixing and so few legitimately concerned to make the right efforts to resolve crisis enigmas. With so many dead and or dying there is almost no time to commit to a quality good job we are in dire straits and it keeps getting worse the challenge has made itself the elephant in the compact. We cannot afford minimal sluggish solutions our pace to succeed has to be commensurate with our drive will power to overcome obstacles to succeed is tantamount to paramount.

I have to be wary skeptical of anyone in this the same nation that slaughtered Buffalo to extinction and Indigenous same place where "White man speak with forked tongue," sold slaves on auction blocks separated races in communities we cannot escape the damages machinations of the past to adorn our futures with lies. If anyone is talking about real solutions and don't start at failed Reconstruction post emancipation you are barking up the wrong tree look you haven't got a clue how far we have not come since multiracial Seneca Falls. A triumph of cultural growth then the lynchings throughout the south and Midwest of the early 1900s they have never admitted real numbers some of my family had to fall victims for we hail from Virginia and Georgia the peach of Election 2020. Now imagine the real number of black women raped and killed same time period they outnumber lynchings I bet stake on it Tuskegee experiment or southern black women forced to have uterus removed or how about years of back alley coat hanger abortions our societal fix for unconscionable generations of favoring white solvency. Appeasing cultural expectations by limiting opportunities to those least fortunate but more capable of progressive viability and granting opportunity to inconsiderate opulence privileged who vehemently profoundly are more apt to abuse it college entrance acceptance classic example insider trading influencing even our most enamored stars. Palm greasing in Congress or Senate the number of good but unfortunate souls given wrong treatments in medical facilities or Lobotomy procedures on sane but poor. Human trafficking sex slavery body part abduction we are a country awaiting the next appearance of serial killer mass murderer where it's ok for a 15-year-old with a stolen assault rifle to drive two states and shoot kill two unarmed victims then extolled by Trumpdemic the flatulent Him he who allowed it to flourish. Healing is inadequate in scope of enigmatic schema problem solving using more conceptual path to clear straight thinking solutions far from easy ginormous daunting as a task nation unification around a central theme contouring cultural intellectualism to encompass provocative use of materials to formulate a construct able to generate massive public change similar to healing remedy. In fact acceptable working compromise universally preferred to narcissistic violent anarchy use the same tools TV to educate the medium is the message and the massage and demonstrate the power TV has to influence. Show how hero's like Stacey Abrams can be assaulted by ignorance in use of words name calling another area of male dominant testosterone bullying glass ceiling income disparity disadvantage. If you want to know about skeletons in the closet how about a country that would deny access to our port turn around orders givent o two large German passenger ships filled with Jewish families knowing no other countries would accept them in 1944 returning to Germany was fatal for everyone on board yet we rename our culture not Anglo-Saxon protestant but hypocrisy in renaming it Judeo Christian no offense to anyone and oh by the way what's up with LGBT the society and culture is so remarkably childish we struggle to acculturate what should be a feature of already accepted society like normal marriage. To fix all this we should seek outside help this is too much for this one even God might have to partner up.

Why are we still threatened by 1 crazy mad white fart a birth his mamma tried to forget? Let's just call him and accident work in progress with all the tools at our disposal to dispose of chaff caustic barf bellowing snotty arid odors the result of not tending to an open wound allowing infection to set in fetid now and spreading. His antics now responsible for 5 deaths there is so much blood on this orange-white Russian man's hands somewhere around one hundred thousand plus 5. Why aren't we rid of this obvious menace yet? Seems so hard to knock off this white joke but a person of color would have been short work. We should not be stuck with a mass murderer posing as POTUS. Streamline procedures and processes to fix the shabby machinations propped-up constraints of elected leaders.

I want to discuss indoctrination in detail to connection with radicalization normalized routines daily behaviors regimen not regime whether assimilation or acculturated. Beliefs are shaped by parental rearing upbringing or lack of it dynamics relevant to our current nationwide dilemma once after hopefully successful diaper training allowed freedom to learn through play educate acquire job skills development of confidence build coping mechanisms socialize form relationships find meaning of life in friends charity concern for others. Missing in those whose parenting might have been compromised by misfortune I understand this as a firsthand witness I had 1 chance as a 12-year-old to go to a Christian summer camp we stopped at Lark Ellen Home for orphaned young boys and took a compliment with us to Big

Pines Summer Camp in the San Bernardino Mountains. We bonded through multiple multiracial multicultural recreational activities pure joy for a couped up adolescent. One incident in the common dining room happened at a table shared by eight diners it was polite to break your bread when offered reminded of it when forgotten. An orphan used 1/2 a stick of butter on his slice of bread he was cautioned of the waste absence of need admonished for denying others he was excessively verbally recalcitrant punished summarily he took temporary solace in what he thought was funny it was just sad because he had the same potential for acceptance then he became verbally caustic unbecoming. I don't know if he was willing to comprehend good behavior socialized to be compatible but I knew he was capable of it. Indoctrination by itself can be learning a trade religion internship apprenticeship degree scholarship moral equivalent of ok honorable requires determination dedication sacrifice forming priorities goal oriented endeavors to succeed typical to dreams ascribed. Radicalization in form or substance is a self-inflicted impetus to achieve goals derived from altered states not enough to suggest masochism explains everything fringe questionable distorted confused too often deranged suspect subject to criminal coincidence the latter also being self-motivated these behaviors temporary permanent or extreme are problematic. Usually narrow in scope of focus resistance to clear reasoning deriving purpose from twisted logic relevant to intolerance repression starving out truth for some mentally disfigured form of redemption through radicalization of conceptual worth through ascendancy of failed self ready to be shared to attract membership. Only to arrive at a pillar alter of scars worshipped as renegade heretics seeking justification like ages old artifact unearthed obelisk inappropriate dangerous regimen beyond control those marred by this pit of despair can change but the desire has to exist to pursue corrective endeavor. First shed bonds of self-limitations to reckon with past mistakes which expose inadequacies able to be restructured reinforcing societal compatibility and a desire to belong to something greater. By working together to contour cultivate a graphic construct outlining the course offering massive social change having the ability to get along with others is priceless not universally shared thereby it may be necessary to lose jealousy envy lust greed. People become disgruntled for lack of a better way we make our own future helping each other get there safely is preferable to oblivion through self-annihilation move over rover let Jimmy take over we can't go back from where we came the way forward is etched with pain shamefully sick lame.

I am horrified by the images of joy being promoted exuded through Trump Jr. video of results of machinations lies of his daddy and Gugglianiani trial by combat this insurrectionist insane inane participation is traitorous contagion witnessed in the room as the POTUS gleefully watches mental deficients like Him he who allowed it to flourish rampaging out of control threatening Democracy and lives. Exhibiting murderous actions knowing possible consequences of their inciteful language and not caring one bit drinking dancing laughing at the armed freak chaos they started but cowardly remained aloof sheltered in the People's House handing out pain as sustenance making you like it and beg for more madness openly displayed without concern for legal consequences alarming to say the very least they must be stopped.

Stop it, please, right now. No more Mr. Nice guy. No one should side with or condone the apparent actions of this seditious rebellion. Leaders much like laws related to gangs you were there you share guilt of causal coconspirator in addition GOP senator Blunt such a creepy old school stale muffin stud gone out of 'em puffing, "he touched the hot stove once and he won't do it again," throw this if it ain't broke hound dog out of the office he holds on his head. It might encourage better thinking in this miserable failure of a legislative senatorial representative and others like him. Expose this same old same old we got to put it behind us cut the umbilical connection to insurrectionists and feed it to them.

What it is? What is it really the exhibitionist rioters want to achieve storming the legislative capitol? If they had harmed members of legislative branch which one how many to what purpose do you accost or threaten or maim? How would repercussions of such tyranny placate heathen savage carnage? What ethics values morals would survive? What kind of place would that be like? What social structure would they assemble as a murderous alternative something out of the black-and-white scenes in new-age raw ruthless movies impossible to sustain no option for continuity recipe for human final failures a tragic end to such a noble valiant collective effort of generational sacrifice because you see truth is it doesn't stop here it's worldwide in every nation just as formidable as an impending extinction event you better ask somebody?

With our futures in so much jeopardy it stands to reason working to secure multiple options for curative venue are cynosure centered on fixes leaving nothing off the table. Now consider an emergency so menacing sojourn of Quantum ship may present a last hope for our continuing existence here post pandemic revolt insurrection calamity. A visit to the past to introduce a bioengineered reagent into earth atmosphere at a precise moment in time to maximize remedy to ease the pain of collision with inevitability like it or not we have to give it all we got take our best shot put it all on the line we are running short on time we late out the gate in direction we make right from the start this is going to take heart.

Those in charge Joint Chiefs of Staff, CIA, FBI, Military Intelligence, NSA, HMLDS, internal affairs all have discussed issue and outcomes of the influence of service and wartime contributions to our wounded Veterans victims scarred for life now must be considered in a different light angered outraged insulted that they are unable to utilize a get everything you want free card grinding heads against the very institutions you fought to defend once you have served and the adventure comes to an end now don't say it wasn't you could get training try your hand at killing the enemy perfect your techniques for successful incursion then abruptly you are done out back on the street job credentials required you have to face change which involves nonviolence incorporating civility but you miss the action seeking it out still like an addiction shooting a gun at a range not cutting it what then? Militia brings promise of redo for some of tactics battle action depending on your brother in the field you join bond train and wait join every conspiracy theory cult to belong estranged stray being domesticated by intelligent trouble makers. Filling a void bottomless pit of hatted desire to see suffering because it brings back feelings of self-worth lost to broken men in pieces due to broken promises. Props to all these victims for you truly have been manipulated through personal sacrifice but I owe you one thing reinforcing the dream for which service for some meant not coming back being that American that fits into the apple pie piece of this puzzle working paying taxes living communally nonviolent law abiding helping others to participate as well moving forward the goal better quality of life for you and yours me too so I routinely include the disrupters seen storming our American Dream on January 6 in my concept of these United States. Although we cannot set the past aside we can learn from it ameliorate our future perspectives with understanding soon technology will be able to provide enough recreational nuances spaceage Halodecks tech challenging satisfying reckless even hardcore rabble rousers. Rebels native sons that think this country owes them something well get in line Uncle Sam owes us all big time but we are all expendable standing in the way of progress the choice is yours get on board live in peace drop the facade let go of old struggles battles long gone and settled face the new battle challenge a life of fulfillment of tolerance achievement wisdom charity faith fellowship cross social boundaries never there marginal friendships cherished relationships. In other words do you start to get my gist make it your place to join the Human Race.

All I'm gettin' here with six days left on this C ticket ride is this ruckus is exactly what Mighty Whitey wanted all of us undesirables to see witness there machination power to toss it up and avoid consequences that we don't have the luxury to elude well I'm not buying it I ain't never scared and that fugitive from a good guy Moscow Mitch Russian troglodyte making a public display of partisanship moving a rapid tide to impeachment numbah dos I'm not buying it too unfamiliar too little too late 2 out of 212 not ready to condemn coup most of Congress and Senate unsuitable for civilized legislative representation, however this winds up they got what they wanted exhibitionist attention from power aspired to but not within reach chasing a pipe dream causing a ruckus amongst us in denial seeking retribution for their own pitiful failures worthless malignant impeding Liberty this can't be what you want the ghosts of centuries upended turning over in their graves condemning us all to a slow death we might as well be damned but I'll be damned if the U.S. is just going to let it happen don't trip don't get sore be careful what you wish for.

There's an energy here that keeps us going you can tap into with the know how some call it positive hope faith charity knowledge wisdom maturity drive will power motivational not just the spark synapse in your cerebellum that is akin to your soul all around us ebbing flowing moving force unequaled if you are apart of this you got to know how to go with the flow swimming against current is for the experienced you could drown for lack of it not complicated or rocket science the immense beauty of moving past castles made of sand time inharmonic balance with your every move you are swept up inundated immersed an adventure you are plugged in rotating positioning the wind sun moon surf a sunrise electric as I become a particle on a wave surreal magnificent thrilling a rush like not many others no concept of stress, oh, the hell with the rest this day is the best so a mental gain I took the pain to write my name on the ocean a sea of love just like from heaven above unlimited accessible to everyone most anytime freedom can be sampled in many unique forms lots of which are still free no expenses to commune with nature seek the metaphysical to cure the aberrations of critical sociopolitical resolute to welcome the new day make good trespass to find a new way.

Now he's gone and done it only POTUS in history Trumpdemic the flatulent Him he who allowed it to flourish has made the Class of Lowdown but impeached twice in the House of Representatives now lives in infamy a legend in his own stolen from us time forever now known till time is no more as the Trump gambit fuckapresidencyup. Sho 'nuff wack to me, yessiree bob.

We are already in a dire position closures no large gatherings social distancing mandate our lives are in restraint under serious restrictions undesirable, however necessary the unhinged nihilistic behaviors witnessed by decent Americans has served to function as a zip tie tethering us to more imposed reductions in the ways we can conduct business closure of the National Mall. As long as I can remember Inaugural Ceremonies have been attended by public large gleeful crowds observing one of the wonders of the world transition of power Obama had probably the largest public gathering in our history but I was more impressed early on by my personal favorite President of our history JFK whose inaugural address lives in infamy like John and Jackie Barack and Michelle were the powerful image makers glorious to have witnessed now tragically soured perhaps permanently by the understanding unpatriotic selfish anarchist angry at the failures they have become trampled our American Capitol ruining the age-old ceremony for fear of armed rebel confrontations this atrocious out of control stupidly has destroyed it for everyone else. Our country looks like a fascist autocracy armed troops in cities to maintain flow of daily business very uncomfortable inconvenient as there are now lots more white males on our streets carrying assault weapons the Trump machinations plague on our lives is permanent as more changes happen in our lives to manage extremism ineptitude brutish vile despicable glutenous self-aggrandizement perpetrated by wealthy to incite braindead racists to tear it all down while they drink dance and take selfies this makes the road ahead look bleak desolate dangerous tentative for the enemy from within our nation has wealthy benefactors patrons willing to sponsor sedition govt. needs to set up roadblocks to carnage crippling use of chaos to regain our dominance as road warriors in the nonviolent pursuit of lives entitled to better than this broken down 1-man no show here we go yo.

This is not a joke. Does someone think this is funny? I don't. It seems the disenfranchised showoffs may have gotten what they wanted an unexpected unintended unforeseen unanticipated undulated undesirable unwanted unwarranted unavoidable unreasonable outcome armed presence in our free streets white men armed with assault weapons to undoubtedly protect the mighty white parents grandparents guardians in their modestly outfitted fortresses from the likes of everyday non-whites from hiking to get prescriptions food and supplies to join a bread line or soup kitchen seek community food banks go to a park with kids so much endangers the paranoid elite they stumble over their own feet the dreary nature of this deceit treacherous complex corrupt devious pias who is to say how many legislative law makers are responsible for aiding and abetting dismemberment of our very way of life. It was already tough here hard to handle for some fatal now on every street corner a reminder of our inability to focus in on real threat and execute effectual universally celebrated homeostasis for the good of us all. All for one and one for all. We cannot afford to forget this wisdom: "Ask not what your country can do for you, ask what you can do for your country." This is an embarrassing fall from grace not the fault of most get up dust ourselves off and revisit strength through unity of Democratic practice let's go for it not because it's easy but because it's hard.

Who's the bigger baby? Rightwing terrorist extremists or the needy hardworking poor seeking more than just survival but marginal upward mobility strides to successful quality of life paths. RWT are morbid racists pampered spoiled with scope of white privilege dangerous destructive mean inconsiderate twisted fragmented mentalities sociopaths their chosen paths are murderous intolerable unsustainable in rhetoric and disheveled distorted disfigured monomaniacal reality a harmful detriment to themselves and others. RWT typically disguised as a neighbor but with heinous intent not seen until dangerous as a crowd to witness AOC saying she was in peril and feared for her life even from colleagues is trauma to be avoided valuable lawmakers need to be protected at all cost. Exposure of RWT is disabled by opportunists we need a national strategy to hogtie these swine and separate them mark them to bring into full rebellious view a whitewash movement a Tom Sawyer paint the fence strategy no weapons in response to their exhibitionist displays of assault gear just balloons filled with white paint to be used a nonviolent effort to label the perpetrators they would leave a mark not harmful but the harm would be felt by numbers in response participation time to white wash away the pain stain of racism to clean up the act.

Let the games begin a phrase interpreted from Roman and Greek historical literature athletic competition passed down through the ages in European culture games of thrones the game is afoot gaming rivalry incentivized by economic cultural differences adding diversity Rubik's cube three-dimensional chess monopoly Nintendo Mario Bros. Farmville centipede interweaving recreation skill challenge stress relief a game needs players providing unique outcomes prowess our need to overcome adversity at this time of 6 pandemics virus deaths new cases hospitals outgunned closures Trumpdemic sparked January 6 it's game on game over are we game to admit we ain't playing no games here don't you see we got game to be on our best game I got game you got game he got game she got game they got game don't you see here's the game to be on our best game.

Majority rules is a far cry from mob mentality. On video after video mostly white people in various forms of defensive protective clothing shields weapons chemical agents they came to cause havoc exhibitionists losing control of civil restraint using violence property damage as a statement of vented disgust marring permanently government institutions unjustified heathen savagery imbecilic rage incited by perpetrators clinging to fantasy a veritable *Lord of the Flies* white privileges disdainful use of inane illegitimate lies to corrupt sinister beliefs in dominance through racism repression subversion of Democracy for acquisition of autocracy which if it succeeded would cause decline of western civilization in favor of murderous corrupted culture self-destructing as they are trapped in power-feeding frenzy once having rendered opposition mute they become expendable useless in the way obstacles to power gorging the paranoid dilemma a future unsustainable no increase in growth untimely dwindling populations deluged by tragedy eventually control freaks will reduce us to no births as destruction of multiethnic cultures doom all of mankind recognizing this could bring us to understand that our time remaining here on earth is now able to be calculated to the last individual and the last minute the calculation currently looks like less than 200 years cold hard reality is half the planet seems to want it. Rioter paradise is it really destroy murder then drinking braggadocios laughing with fellow lawbreakers then planning more reality is these nuts have too much free time guidance is a requirement for this type of mental retardation for this behavior is not socially redeemable where does that leave us between the administration and a bunch of crazies trying to kill Democracy us then eat each other try not to choke on this as appetizer bon appetit.

Everything around us that we look at is looking more and more like a B disaster movie with stars you think no you know you have seen before threats coming from every direction survivors challenged to find solutions while the dying is panicky abundant desperate people trying to save their lives under duress of suffering lose no solutions in sight hospitals overcrowded morgues overflowing body bags piling up a few years ago I speculated on a Crematorium as a business now as I see these conditions wow there would be no shortage of customers and mega worldwide demand increasing daily minute by minute so how about that vaccine distribution schedule that governors cross the country are complaining is derelict no stock supply to even accomplish second doses already in process still bogged down by federal neglect failures of procedural management incompetence obstructing quick action needed now more than ever before in modern history as our crisis now exceeds all others short of the extinction event impact in

South America which did in 90 percent of all life we are up against it this one will forge then write a new chapter in the annals of human survival conservative or not perhaps now is the time to use every option take every risk use every measure incorporate all shortcuts and prioritize finding more we are faced with ginormous daunting task fix the pandemic get public health back open culture rebuild society job expansions legislative attack on failed government institutions and representatives rebuild trade and economic growth but the longest yard will be the ball and chain worn by all repatriation of diehard addicted to guns gunpowder on the brain stupid ass backwards whiny exhibitionist narcissist mentally disfigured retarded fuckheads.

I have a path to endeavor to follow travel along goal oriented a sojourn to a destination some might refer to as a dream I am grateful for the dreamscapes that have freed me up from rigors provided by overindulgence with stress common to trying to scrape yourself off the curb obstacles to travel have handed out detours some dead ends even lost time becoming more crucial valuable staying in my lane cruising paying attention to road hazards although transportation has been helpful not everything required to make this journey the challenges always grow as wisdom renavigates impetus to chart a viable course direct without drama. I can't live a dream for me that is a fantasy I can embrace the dream of others especially internationally known respected for they are equivalent to desired outcome 1 hail from brethren oppressed by years of hatred my very being honed tempered by survival restraints regimen to maintain dignity and composure despite stigma posing danger in any moment of every day kind of a drag you get used to it kinda try to make the best of bad rap but like it or not trouble will make a special effort sometime to instigate headaches unpleasant encounters with belligerence there are many paths to essentially where you want to be thinking outside of the box can keep you in stride. I have incorporated the knowledge a lot can be learned when standing on the shoulders of giants some of which can also be learned by simply climbing a tree or ladder. I am encouraged to know a lot of us seek similar phenomena essential to most peace shelter sanctuary room to grow even the most bloodthirsty culture signed the Pax Romana. Biden does not have to cross the Rubicon but his task is no less formidable for the contents of closet were just revealed outing vile enablers skeletons of past failures perpetuating the fall of America so many worked so hard for this experiment too many have sacrificed for the efforts to collapse the way forward is all too clear we fix the American way brick by brick stone by stone till we can once again really call it home.

RESOLUTION

There is absolutely unmistakably without a shadow of a doubt no way in hell we could get over the multiple dilemma this one is going to leave a mark gowan spread out like after being backhanded by Moe Howard what's really going on here the whackcastrophy anathema plagued our nation damage to linger on still representing the fight for our lives the soul of a nation civil reintegration the lasting stench of modernity deaths due to COVID-19 death of our heritage attacks taking its toll on our demeanor spirit fortitude the last sleepless night under federal assault devouring our governance vomiting molestation of patriotic Democratic resolve devastating seen juxtaposed in coincidence with pandemic crisis federal dereliction of vital Constitutional curative responsibilities now claiming over 200,000 lives Trump and cohorts directly faulted rightfully so in full view of the world the POTUS who would be king bore his big wide fat ass whiff unmistakable like death wafting lingering in our atmosphere trying to stir up turbulence to rock the baby out of the cradle throw it away with the bath water many on a mission to see how they hustles groove we got to be muscle on a mission to make that hustle move we know they had bats in the coup bustin' out the roof wait a minute you no that it's the truth we got to stop the playa hater till the love becomes greater sooner or later stop the player haters we are the originators Biden Harris the motivators till in every generation now or later the love becomes greater.

Great day in the morning. The moments we have been waiting for may the Biden Harris administration provide the leadership necessary to fix all creation heal our nation.

Change has to be verbally communicated correctly to be able to visualize the progress of the process news reporting should be wary of the scope of suggesting Americans all celebrate change in Administration when past voter and insurrectionist exhibition display half the country tonight feels pushed aside disabled not represented not going to be eliminated by threat or force people everywhere for this to work we have to be on the same page we all have to admit fault just as we must all want to heal set devious personal motives for harm aside to favor recovery from this fast becoming extinction event can't get too comfortable because crazy ain't always lazy is contagious and difficult to reign in. Passion once again flows pulsating through the veins of a nation held prisoner by negativity hope springs eternal liberty once again within our grasp hurdles ahead we have trained for clearing each one confidence restored in the right path regained the Moral Arc of history and justice wait in judgment of what is to come write and execute the play book to score victories in completed plays bring it on back no middle of the night just plain black and white do what you like but let's get this right we must be clear about every statement course of action taken to remedy by acceptable compromise our meanings and messages must be succinct to the point not candid or suspect healing must be apparent in attempt and purpose our lives now different we have now seen what has been revealed in contents of closet and what it represents war of stupidity uncivil flaunted by uncivilized atrocious excuses for human beings let me ask you. If you could Bernie Mac bitch slap all the participants of January 6 is there 1 in the bunch you would not slap? I would give up sleep to get that job expedited the cat is out of the bag Pandora's box is open ready or not you can't hide there is nowhere to escape. Are we dealing with people who cannot or won't extend their best to work together? Read my lips this is not a childish rivalry our best is yet the only alternative to get back to how we want to live being the best we can be.

Now it's time to come along and join our family hey there hi there ho there you're as welcome as can be forever let us hold our banner high come along sing our song join the family remember this stuff happiest place on earth snap fucking out of it time the ugly truth comes out Disneyland employees trajically underpaid. Certain civilians live believe put faith in the aberrated irrational dogma that the code of the south pre-Civil War delusional proprietary pursuit of sole racial mastery dominance through submission perversion of ethics morally corrupted aims of supremism everything else exist to serve at their convenience needless to say sheer tragic insanity incontrovertible madness those people run free daily to in blind rage attack blame us for wanting to put distance from atrocity nursing ghosts of the dream long dead back to health giving in to savagery imbecilic apocastrophic enigma seeing yourself as a union rebel son and daughter instead of admitting the northern triumph over adversity and that means now you are a native son distinguished by perseverance valor truth justice sorry to say abhorrent to supremism there is only middle ground if you allow it closed minds are a wrench in the works no easy quick fix gorilla glue ain't going to cut it using it properly or sniffed although I tend to think many sniffed too much paint alcoholism can't cause that type of dementia drug use imbalance in physical make up can contribute to mental retardation guiding daily lives. Such a deluded character is resistant to peaceful transitions infectious dangerous lying in wait a predator that would kill for their own comfort and satisfaction and teach the same perverted aspersions to others. How to get comfortable in the lion's den while awaiting explanation of lodgings? This might be a good time to panic yell for help loudly loud as we can loud enough to be heard loud as can be to wake this KKK kind of beast up sheets over their heads aren't needed anymore as they have allies in Congress and the Senate law enforcement military bureaucracies brutes evolving in reverse losing the ability to reason reduced to baser instincts which would explain the feces at the Capitol Hill sharing the planet is becoming less and less attractive perhaps the solution could not be seen for the trees simpler than believed divide the planet give them habitat at the bottom of the ocean. Build an environment where their kind can feel victorious that they have won separatism and let everyone wants to go get gone logistics of this would be incredible but worth it never the twain shall meet good riddance see yah wouldn't want to be yah. This direct approach no matter how silly you might think may prevent a real second un-civil war 200 years of efforts have not extinguished flames fires of hatred. As this fetid decaying mentality permeates our culture it causes disfigurement killing us softly little by little maybe to be stronger is to allow America to fail the American Way can live on with those ready and willing to make the commitment to excellence pride patriotism Americanism.

America the beautiful god shed his love on the glorification of a dream shared by many worthy inspired intrepid flawed from the git-go born of revolutionary resolve longed for idealism honor bound in traditions heritage hope fraught with malice aforethought defeated on the battleground but not in ideology prefaced by irrational devious bias perverted entrenched in southern culture we brought our current dilemma on ourselves knowing the minds of confederate die-hards would survive social extremes tied to generations of family heritage not good enough to say our bad this failure to address repatriation reconstruction has snowballed into the mushroom cloud of white supremacists threatening democracy can't say I told you so because I wasn't born when indoctrination into northern culture should have begun anticipating the former enemy would be recalcitrant. The federal government is directly responsible for lack of focused long-term industrialized financial support programs attitude adjustment programs to facilitate long-term servility and acculturation of diehard fatalistic extremist exhibitionist reluctant to sever the umbilical connection to insurrectionism thus there daily existence is guerrilla warfare handed down from father to son mother to daughter. Sinister plays a part in all of this lunacy barbarism makes up the bulk. Hold up wait a minute can't we fix this whack stuff mend it? Two hundred years of doing the same things unite America despite opposition to it struggles with potential brush with crazy come on we are better than this seek finality with these fugitives from federal lock down let them go work on a system to develop regional barriers worst example east and west Germany crucial solutions to not being able to live in peace with these opportunistic extortionist extremists. Regrettable I have done favors for good ole boys to better their lives and vice versa I respected the common struggles I had their backs in street brawls fights I take pride in because we held our own this shit goes much deeper. White people should not feel imprisoned in foundations of America if it doesn't work for them they have a right to seek out remedies short of violence. Country posed to work for everybody. So where does this leave us? After 200 years where do we go from here? What the fuck how about this for dumb luck? Threshold to paradise and those Smucks won't play nice.

I guess I've about had it. There are many current mainstream political efforts to address sociopolitical issues and outcomes still focused on unification over 200 years things amounting to getting much worse is this not the very definition of insanity? Why! Please say there's another way. Our lives are forfeit to the detriment of murderous extremism a real drag obstacles to a good life conceived and imagined earned by dedication to continuity of pursuit of promise to progress and not evolve in regress. Lives are now put on hold as we all float in a massive school on the viral sea of carnage aided by inadequacies in curative procedures now dominated by death and infection or mortality rates unprecedented in history as we fight in every way possible to stay afloat the absence of life-saving remedy crisis building to insurmountable. Clear what has to be prioritized but without the benefit of logical function in previous administration we are literally starting from scratch. Time is a wasting I'm a hankering itchin' to get back to do this to do that eat a damn chili weinie and drink a good martini creme brulee tiramisu flan mole guacamole margaritas Ole'! Back to the point what, how, when, where, which, methods will be the most immediately effective to address an age-old problem swept under the rug for generations fooling ourselves decade after decade in false Band-Aid type bad of bad thinking narrow in scope in denial of magnitude of machinations ultimate fate of the American experiment using every means not to admit failure when we have transplanted so many body parts to keep rebuilding our nation it parallels the work done on the Frankenstein creation. Let it go. First we got to fix this mess here. To do so would free up our lives to once again soar free survivors of multiple pandemics one being human enemy. Then there has to be a better way to problem solve unification failures perhaps the media continually referring to Earth Two might be more significant as mass relocation might eventually be equated as our freedom and salvation.

Here is something a Sunday thought might query, the January 6th Vigilante Mob attacking the Capitol spell out hypocrisy. How many of those lying ornery cuss say they are honest in pursuit of faith and pray to their creator of their antagonistic assault attacking purpose just senseless killing and maim? What it's ok to sin if fetish wins? Sin is a matter of opinion profitable in fact for some misinterpretation allowing attention to be diluted through dubious misunderstanding useful in bending flexing social boundaries when viewed though the microscope allow access income for some shielded from criminal blame immunity granted to wealthy privileged able to exploit the most extremism for profit and personal gain in contrast indifference to most outside the perimeter range of establishment privilege. Ask the Russian mafia how well their photo model businesses are doing at present compared to recent past. I don't think Larry Flint is short of on cash or model applicants. Porn industry is not losing money poor Ukrainian women our efforts to massage Putin's ego has had a negative counter effect on their opportunities and the valley is still valley girls back page from the alley can't say the effects of deprivation deviant altering our society and culture aren't useful in corrupting morals and values destroying the age of innocence preferring instead the lust-driven goal of exploitation in condemnation of conservative to mid-range social regularity inhibiting normalcy in male female relationships reversing the male dominance handicap but sacrificing spontaneity as income becomes an issue in natural selection almost to the point of being an oxymoron. To quote King Kunta: "life ain't nuttin' but a phat vagina." Now thinking that most of the perpetrators augment their incomes with sales of drugs contraband guns explosives the culture they would assemble if succession enabled would undoubtedly be lawless extreme not survivable doomed to self-destruction. Better them I say we give them the ropes let them hang themselves. Popcorn, anyone?

A normal response to greetings coming at me as far back as I can remember has been "I'm tryin' to keep from dyin'" years of running the gauntlets Venice Beach Santa Monica seashores Malibu Ventura Oxnard Manhattan and Redondo Beach my favorite breaks came at Seal and Huntington Beach Torrance East LA Inglewood and South Central going anywhere places off limits seem to beckon adventure endless summer running out of time now to be enjoyed by others as the extremes of decades have eroded our society and culture so much more is lost in history as we have lost normalcy convenience social gathering friends family exhausted frustrated angry disillusioned but as we continue on into our unforeseen possible future if existence ever more critical than before we are all tryin' to keep from dyin'.

I have a thought now be silent those of you who warn deem I'm incapable of it. We have lots lots of common problems struggles with a toxic noxious planetary super virus currently kicking all our asses with government bureaucratic institutional inadequacies some bordering incompetence leading the charge up Valley Forge it all seems to be as inept as Custer's Last Stand. No offense to any fans but do you want to know dark if the virus goes mega super ballistic spread unstoppable they will consider Smart Nuke strikes to eliminate super infection zones causing disastrous civilian consequences and outcomes. I hope we won't get to this point where daily we see people collapsing on the streets and being unable to stop and offer life-saving assistance over concerns of infection. Cities have relaxed restrictions on air quality as crematoriums are working 24-7 and can't keep pace with incoming volume soon we may smell this daily as demands increase 2021 and these conditions mirror those during the murderous Black Plague which decimated Europe. Visibility has improved as a result of the current enigmas revealing our gorgeous ambient weather strata but also machinations criminal intent carnage chaos thievery litigious gauging out of foundational structures by notorious ambivalent scoundrels celebrating their exposure now and forever known as diabolical. We are pawns on a worldwide game board skaters taking a jump carving a rail getting air and flipping out quarterbacking our own play books shooting the waves curls in this world then you see a girl who rocks your world don't hurl haven't lost my mind just rhyme to find the time to reflect what the heck great Caesar's ghost monopoly straw dogs leap frogs debauchery mockery vehement chaff abrasive in denial of disfunction needing to reconnect with Conjunction Junction what's your function arrive at the intersection of stay alive survival of the fittest not skittish confident content to prevent lament come around both feet on the ground get down dirty hurdy hurdy gurdy gurdy keep singing songs of love.

Dear President Biden-Vice President Harris: The time is now to make bold steps to manage regulate plan effective remedies to multiple existential threat to our nation. In consideration of the vigor witnessed by your phenomenal winning campaign strategies to retrofit our American policies and vital to commitments make up for the damage caused by previous administration. Your targeted efforts in the first days of leadership are restoring faith in our united resolve. I implore you to manage make water collection, storage, of fresh water resources also a priority since Global warming is progressing unchecked. Ideally I propose a massive government work project to revolutionize our sewage and water collection to target fresh water storage as our most vital resource yearly flows out to sea while east Midwest are flooded while the west is drying out. A reclamation system as a national work project accomplishes water efficiency plans can include sharing water and this can be operated state by state generating urgently needed employment. A design concept that builds a facility in Louisiana below water level goals to catch all fresh water to prevent wasteful drainage to the ocean. Interlacing design features to produce active pipelines to channel water from state to state will ease up natural disasters to our benefit. I have offered this discourse to encourage positive resource solutions. Thank you for your attention. May America continue to be blessed! Should I mail it?

Freedom was never about us against them. A greater concept is conceived when exploration of avenues reveal paths to glory. A dilemma here is rapidly approaching blowout boiling over coming to a head. If half the world strikes out to eliminate the other half of the world do the math that doesn't leave many here not enough to run things. Who in their right mind can be aiming for that outcome? Tomato tomato black with white stripes white with black stripes potato potato wrong is right right is wrong is anyone tired of the same old runabout runaround runaround inside out upside down endless carnival ride into dregs of wannabe's nuts believing their chaotic murderous insidious dreams are born of our demise bent on killing all of us and destroying property to resurrect the insanity of rebel renegades in effect patterns of the corrupt slavery south as theses misfits cannot be satisfied without exercising their perversions to subjugate imprison enslave abuse physically injure torture to get others to beg for mercy their lives an aphrodisiac to supremism. There is little survivable quotient after the mass killing in other words these carnies may spell the end of mankind even though most are drug crazed and most likely illiterate. Freedom is twisted or demented but inspirational desirable sought after deemed worthy of most deliberate efforts achievement comparable equated often as a feeling of happiness wellbeing security comfort satisfying and so much more. I could make a two hundred word sentence and only scratch the surface of schema associated with freedom. A defining difference may lend the ultimate understanding my concept of freedom does not involve their death and destruction this is not reciprocal to have their way is for us to die the battle lines have been drawn. There may be no other way but to give them what they want lending to feeling sorry for those mental deficits for it is no contest as intelligent will easily vanquish lack of it. Any outcomes of this scenario are extinction for enough will be lost to render viable populations null. Aftermath, anyone?

Knowledge is power more than integral to a whole well informed person to develop further skills. The perverted proselytic proclivitous murderous personalities are bent on machinations one subversion denial of power not so much money shared wealth on a small scale important to nourish base including multi racial partnerships grim reaper Moscow Mitch married to a Chinese billionaire JZ money and limited power important to racist fascists conservatives compromises necessary for the good ole boys to keep riding. Truth be told power is everything to racist supremist Trumpian ass wipes and they will wax mad dog stink eye crazy to let everyone know like a fart in a small crowded room. When education of slaves became a must the mangy bunch of losers began hating to this day to take away power in every form sustenance income viability self-dignity awareness ownership possession shelter they would deny even spartan extremes. The sheer jealousy insurmountable indecent malevolent is indication of severe mental psychosis shared as a badge of courage in fact misguided disfunction. Seems a waste with so little time to really live our lives riddled by land mines to satisfy their personal cravings. What next? Whatever it is bring it sooner we can mop the blood of these creeps off our nation sooner we can get on to greatness. What the hell are we waiting for?

What it is? What is it? The aromatic fragrance in the air everywhere you go which use to waft the occasional favorite bacon and eggs coffee tortillas toast burritos burgers fries now strangely mixed with rotten people decaying a result of cult dependence minds corroded stench-ridden egomaniacal nihilism detriment to non-offensive breathing permeating our society and culture similar to cancer but far more deadly destructive potentials like a primitive life form waiting to gobble us all up self-inflicting its own end by eating its own tail hard to admit as much as I despise cops that my eyes teared up as a police officer lies in state a result of the failed coup Jan. 6 attempt at hostile takeover in our lifetime on live TV devoid of any sense incapable of feigning intellect a rouse deception nothing atypical of egomaniacal narcissism braindead in effect walking talking dead morbid noxious profane indecent yougooly ugly immoral ill-conceived illin ill-equipped illicit lame excuses a plague pox deadly variant offensive horrible by design colorful input check the rhyme press rewind.

There is an inherent problem with life conception being born life launched learning to live. Problem is "we do not place a high enough moral or value standard level on the living." Something happened as a result of our continuing presence facing obstacles so many challenges to survival we are damaged our psyche chi characters warped twisted tweaked to the point we have out of desperation lost our grip on resolve giving in to resignation aberrated tolerance for killing or being ok with senseless untimely death and demise. Does this not make all of us painfully sorrowfully reluctantly pathological? The manner in which real life violence vicious murder mayhem drama continuously outpace the Hollywood writers supplying endless scenarios some of which repeat as diabolical life traumas. Let's face reality it's so corrupted here on earth everywhere we are a possible contaminate for other worlds as this madness may be localized inspired here distinct only unknown beyond our planet. After all intelligent creatures having to survive extremes of outer space would develop as primary self and community reliant survival techniques and would have little time to waste killing each other. Now then the machinations actions of a self-centered imbecilic coward and cohorts directly purposefully instigated hostile takeover of the Election while they danced drank took selfies their gang of crazies attacked our institutions and people died horror needlessly tragically painfully in front of the world the great experiment hobbled. To have witnessed the historical dark blemish of Trumpdemic and Trumpistas still rattling vipers ready to strike not hunters just predators wanting carnage working on our obliteration taints the colors of the day.

What? How? When? Why? Questions poignant in consideration of the mackination of alienation tactical oppression targeting specific society and culture with influential results stimulus causally related to continuing escalating turmoil conflicts endangering certain communities and civilians impacting lives negatively. The US thugs mack daddy billionaires deviant corrupted by power delusional as they fill roles they have imposed on us that are akin to being put asunder buried by plate tectonics. The alienation has mutated over time like this deadly virus as the white mack daddy effect matures bends and flexes currently tolerated as a nuisance like a tablespoon of castor oil or an enema or intravenous. Challenged as we already were now that we are shut down crippled stagnant trudging along powering through clumsy change of govt. was imperative now viral containment and economic recovery are prioritized then there is business growth and development fixing broken legislation getting back to what was if existence. Complex problems that were scorched earth before these crisis are now thermonuclear alienation in so many conflictual schemas is rampant rampaging now it seems our vital social issues will take more of a back burner than ever before. As one national crisis after another piles our plates higher it is plain to see there is no fix there is no revealing of a real road to healing normalcy will be to regain flow status quo typical neglect resultant redirect sympathy but no remedy. The task is too great requires comprehensive planning follow through daunting mandating permanent solutions to enigma reclassified for the sake of convenience to erase the shame of failure to supply working solutions in support of communities of color. It boils down to we are in it all alone they will throw us all a bone tell us there is nothing to see here have no fear send us home.

Why people of color? You say go back to where you come from. You say you hate Moslem Black Latino Indigenous Asian Mongolian Aborigine no you don't. Liars you are too maligned to know any. Only what you have scoured in dark places perused in dank corners siphoned from scars of old wounds sore losers jealous because you lost hate gleaned from obsession repeated out of ignorance stubbornness buffoonery morose incognizance devious dubious vile resentful opportunism self-effacing unwilling to share what you covet as intolerable no can do won't have it not a chance out of the question just as France and Spain divided the planet in half each claiming sole right of possession enforced by military might you weirdos demand recognition all natural resources are your in by right of white parental lineage bonafide selfish needy rebel sons and daughters in fact defiant toxic native sons party poopers took to festering mean and nasty soured shriveled up downright ornery snarling snapping just because you like grey color of the rebel call of the south can't stand sight of Yankee blue too namby-pamby gay polished to much like a negro slave or other 'n word this really has nothing at all to do with ethnicity race politics even gender this is about preference for flying the flag rebel colors of the cause culpable juvenile sad sick a belief that makes them all tricks on the street selling their meat to flip our beat meeting each other to beat one another into defiance primitive in scope day of the jackal followed by the pride of Black History biting them on their pompous asses stalked by destitution incriminated beyond comprehensive embarrassment constant harassment as they try to become omnipotent slip sliding spiral settle nestle right into insanity seek and ye shall find.

If Trump ever wins another election the truth is revealed about this atrociously apologetic fallibly responsible nation having purposely plied the result of human relocation to cause this systemic dysfunctional variation racism generating a side-effect supremism permanently damaging the psycho cohesion of the sociopolitical fabric of a modern society. His their victory will be nothin' but much much much more of the same. No less than a damn shame.

MUSICAL CONSTRUCT

**Album Cover "The California Boys"
presents Johnny Chevy Country Music**

1
California Country Music

We'll be coming 'round the mountains
'Cross the desert to the shore
Now I don't wonder where we are

We'll be goin' down that region
Bridge that yonder to explore
Now I know just what to do

Well, no matter how you choose
It's just the way you use it
This is California Country Music

California, California, California
Country Music
California, California, California
Country Music

Well, no matter how you choose
It's just the way you use it
This is California Country Music

2
Jukebox Club

You heard the news
Time to throw down
Now we gettin' low down

Follow through with memories of
What I do with you

Making music
Is what we do
That stuff
To move your feet to
Is a little reminder
OF the Jukebox Club

Lean girls
Tight blue jeans
Kind to throw down
Boots get to stompin'
To showdown

Baby be more
And more and more and more

Making music
Is what we do
That stuff
To move your feet to
Is a little reminder
OF the Jukebox Club

3

Blue Horizon

The Sky above me
Will always be there
To share
It's better to be that way

The rain falls around you
The wind blowing
Through your soul
Rocks you in its arms
It's better to be that way

You try this for size
I'll keep my eyes on
The Blue Horizon

The earth beneath your feet
Provides shelter
For your needs
It's better to be that way

You try this for size
I'll keep my eyes on
The Blue Horizon

You try this for size
I'll keep my eyes on
The Blue Horizon

4
Like We Used To

All around here and there
Every day and every where
Listen to what people are sayin'
Toe to toe here we go
Got you now don't you know
Let's just keep on playin'

Let's just keep playin'
Playin' just a little bit louder
I reckon lets
Just keep playin'
Playin' like we used to

When the beat gets hard
And the music gets louder
What are we gonna do
I reckon lets
 Just keep playin'
Like we used to do

All around here and there
Every day and every where
Listen to what people are sayin'
Toe to toe here we go
Got you now don't you know
Let's just keep on playin'

Let's just keep playin'
Playin' like we used to
Let's just keep playin'
'Cause everyone is gonna pull through

When the beat gets hard
And the music gets louder
What are we gonna do
I reckon lets
 Just keep playin'
Like we used to do

Let's just keep playin'

Playin' just a little bit longer
I reckon lets
Just keep playin'
Playin' like we used to

When the beat gets hard
And the music gets longer
What are we gonna do
I reckon lets
Just keep playin'
Like we used to do

5
Great Day

I used to dunk pigtails
In inkwells
While in school
I used to
Playin' hooky and
I used to
Break the rules

These are a
Part of days
Gone by I've
Left them far
Behind
It's a great day
And that's fine

Well, I wanted to
Get to know you
But I wouldn't
Waste my time
With your shouldn't
Oughtas baby and
Your cheap talkin' wine

These are a
Part of days
Gone by I've
Left them far
Behind
It's a great day
And that's fine

6
Albuquerque

The wind blowin'
Clears my mind
And it doesn't
Have a skyline
The streets are
Really clean in
Albuquerque

It's got plenty
Street Lights
Blue sky
Stars at night
Lovers and their
Dreams in
Albuquerque

Dust storm thunder
I don't care
Paper blowing
Through the air
America
Now don't forget
You ain't seen
Nothin' yet

It's got plenty
Street Lights
Blue sky
Stars at night
Lovers and their
Dreams in
Albuquerque

7

Welcome to Springfield, Missouri

That great big pile of rock and dirt before my eyes
Must be the beginning of a new high rise.
What did you think it'd take to make this far you roam?
Must be the beginning of a new one.
Welcome home

Land of opportunity
City of thee
I speak – sing – see
What did you?
Think it'd take
To make this
Far you roam
Must be the beginning
Of a new one
Welcome home

Four hundred decades
Of war and poverty
Six hundred generations
Of hate and misery
What did you?
Think it'd take
To make this
Far you roam
Must be the beginning
Of a new one
Welcome home

8
Wanted Dead or Alive

I'm a black man
I know what's up
He said she said
I give a fuck
Easy does it
I'm all about luck

Have at it
Face in a crowd
Oh, god damn it
Cry out loud

A city lives to kill
A government denies the facts
How can I fight to stay Alive
When there's nowhere to hide
Nowhere to hide when you're
Wanted dead or alive

I'm black, I know I
Hold a grudge you better
Lock and load
I still hold that grudge
Rock and roll

I'm a back woods no-count sucker
Wants to beat the hell
Out of a white no count dirty sucker
Oh well

A city lives to kill
A government denies the facts
How can I fight to stay Alive
When there's nowhere to hide
Nowhere to hide when you're
Wanted dead or alive

9
Sweet Dreams

We all want
Sweet dreams
We all live
Fine Scenes
Whoa, Yeah
We want
Sweet dreams

They don't make 'em
Like you
Anymore
If they did
Ever before

We all need
Sweet dreams
We all need
Fine scenes
Whoa, yeah
We need sweet dreams

They don't make 'em
Like you
Anymore
If they did
Ever before

10
Street Rod

She's fine as a woman
On the streets so mean
She's loud when she's revving
Yeah, she's really clean
Street rod
She's a clean machine
Street rod

She's hot as blazes
In a quarter-mile
She fine when she's running
You just ride and smile
Street rod
She's a clean machine
Street rod

11
Push Come to Shove

Do unto others
What themselves might
Do unto you
Push come to shove
Maybe and might be
Our hearts will guide
Us to

I love the thrills
I always will
They do what they do
I love the thrills
I always will

12
Porn Stars and Presidents

Porn stars and presidents
All over my Friday night
Porn stars and presidents
Taking up too much
Of my life
Porn stars and presidents
Porn stars and presidents
Porn stars and presidents
Somehow it don't seem right

Porn stars and presidents
Things ain't ok, they are both white
Porn stars and presidents
They both slimy but
Both think they right
Porn stars and presidents
Boy, white folks fight
Porn stars and presidents
Porn stars and presidents
Porn stars and presidents
Somehow it don't seem right

Porn stars and presidents
Fuckin' up my Friday night
Porn stars and presidents
Why fight whitey
When you both got rights
Porn stars and presidents
Fuck you both involving me
In your fight
Porn stars and presidents
Porn stars and presidents
Porn stars and presidents
Somehow it don't see right - Repeat

13
Maria

True so true
When I met you
Did not waste dear time
Then I knew
True so true
Only you so fine
True so true
Then I knew
Seek and ye shall find
Maria girl
You got to be mine

I know I'm lost
Paid the cost
Seek and ye shall find
Then I knew only you
Seek and ye shall find
When I met you
True so true
Seek and ye shall find
Maria girl, you got
To be mine

14
It's About Time

I'm a man
 Likes to see freedom
Though in me it's lost
I'm a man
Wants to see peace
No matter what the cost
Damn most vile
Dems and Republicans
Cowards freaks
One and all
It's about time
We the people
Heed this call
It's about time
We Americans
Fix it all
It's about time
We the people
Heed this call
It's about time
We Americans
Fix it all

15
Breakfast in Omaha

I'm going Greyhound Double decker on I-40
As I was searching for someone
I'm a young black man but
Does anyone really care?

Run on down you old hound
I'm a traveling alone
As I was searching for somewhere
Yes, I'm a young black man but
Does anyone really care?

I'm doing favors for some
I'm a feeling my angst
I don't want to rob banks
I'm a feeling more angst
As I was a searching out that dream somewhere
When I ate breakfast in Omaha
I found America there

Run 'em down, you ole hound
You a takin' me home
I'm still a searching for someone
I'm a young black man but
Does anyone really care?

Keep running 'round, you ole hound
Take the reins, you a running home down
I'm still searching for somewhere
As I'm a young black man but
Does anyone really care?

I'm doing favors for some
I'm a feeling my angst
I don't want to rob banks
I'm a feeling more angst
As I was a searching out that dream somewhere
 When I ate breakfast in Omaha
I found America there
When I ate breakfast in Omaha
I found America there
When I ate breakfast in Omaha
I found America there

16
Black What?

Ea, He's a black man
Hatin'
Don't you think?

Oh, He's a black man
Hatin' y'all
Ea, He's a black man
Hatin'
Don't you think?

Oh, He's a black man
Hatin' y'all

Can't make the money
To feed myself much less
My woman 'n youngins
Up to here in monthly bill w
Then oh shit, there's
The tax man
Uncle Sam
Uncle Sam

It seems the government
Wants to rob me
Cops want to kill
Streets threaten every minute
Presidency with wannabe dictator in it

17
BarBQue

Come around to BarBQue
Git around up to BarBQue
Come around together
Get down to BarBQue
Git around up to BarBQue
Come around together

BarBQue
This is the right time for
BarBQue
I need you next to me
BarBQue
This is the right time
BarBQue
I need you next to my heart

Come around to BarBQue
Git around up to BarBQue
Come around together
Get down to BarBQue
Git around up to BarBQue
Come around together

18
YO, TEXAS

Here I go to Texas
I'm a goin' to see my friends
Here I go to Texas
Yo, Texas
I'm a comin'

We flatland roaming in the countryside
As far as the eye can see
Panhandle, Mesa, take a hayride
As far as the eye can see

Here we go to Texas
We all a goin' to see our friends
Here we go to Texas
Yo, Texas
We all a comin'

We ranch hand roping in the countryside
As far as the eye can see
Big sky rough riding on a bull rider
As far as the eye can see

Here we all go to Texas
We all a goin' to see all our friends
Here we all go to Texas
Yo, Texas
We come to meetin'

We long tall riding in the countryside
As far as the eye can see
Lone star state union's great divide
As far as the eye can see

19
Shine on Country Roots

In the daytime
Hay while the sun shines
Making that moonshine
Can't waste no time
Cause I'm
Crazy about that Juice
And I'm bound to country roots
From Richmond to Georgia
Look out boys
Im coming for ya
Cause I'm
Crazy about that juice
And I'm born to country roots

20
Yankee Doodle Dandee

Yankee Doodle Dandee is really mean America obscene
Aberrated doubted Uncle Sam outed subversion
Perversion maniacal dispersion aversion to harmful dangerous
Rhetoric what the heck this shit thick not trying to I found my rhyming
You don't need to be conflicted wicked not to worry I ain't
In no hurry after you I got rhymes mines too no disrespect
Don't be jealous fools props to Ice Cube Snoop MC Ren
Mac 10 50 Cent alright then I strike with all my might
Ain't trying to step to you be like you take nothing from you
Have no fear let me make this clear I'm retired professional
Me my rhymes this here is my second career.
The Great Society let all of us down that's all folks
No more messing around us societal snakes slithering
Democratic processes wither hither tither lean a nation
Without a backbone spineless desolate hatred weaned
Viper sidewinders seem a loathsome means to an end.
As I strike with all my might have no fear let me make this clear
I'm a retired professional me mine my rhymes this here
Is my second career.

The Farmer in the Dell was the text of it
Next-level shit ahead of its time
Hi ho away we go what the hell what is that smell
Illin' chillin' no change in that mind it's a fine
Line between that rhyme vexed next you will find

Time press rewind as I strike with all my might
Have no fear let me make this clear I'm a
Retired professional me mine 'n my rhymes see
This here be my second career

Let's pick this whack-ass bad ass
Full metal crazy-ass military jacket shit apart
Give 'em something to run to
'Cause you know this be the nigga be the cause
Gonna come thru

EPILOGUE

I sincerely hope you found meaning in reading this book. Some of the disparaging comments may have been hard to swallow. I did mean to insult, blame, point the finger at the dissonance of dissidents including the self-aggrandizing megalo maniacal bigoted white supremacist nefarious bullies hellbent on dismantling our precious fragile democracy and those who would support them, many of whom currently serve as US. Senators. Perhaps you will relate to an idea described, a scenario depicted or a memory evoked by the voracity of the text impetus to be more in sync, creative or heightened awareness. I also believe it will be a subject of critical conversations for many more years. My ultimate desire to work on recording the lyrics in the book songs I pray you will find appealing. Thank you for your purchase. Be safe, live well, work together to heal our futures for all the better.

One just one good thing comes from the Trumpistas clown show the most white bunch of pale albino bleached blanched scoured scrubbed opaque pasty powdered painted pompous pussies got together in support of throwing out the white power Ace in the hole the Electoral College it would save a lot of time and thereby loads of money this is of govt. benefit a must for any keen charming intellectual dominion capable of inspirational visionary deeds and actions to strike forth carve forge a more direct less circuitous path to the promise land.

I awoke today to look at the disgraceful conduct of our government and criminal justice processes prisoners across the nation 2-4 times more likely for infection no plans to include prisons in vaccinations then the corrupt consistency of police officers once again no Federal charges in the Tamar Rice murder by police I find this particularly disturbing for if you watched the video of this heinous act clearly a white cop shot a child in his face damn the thought that gave birth to their foul stench-ridden rotten asses in addition COVID 19 vaccinations may extend into years if we don't step up the pace also a new legislator elect just passed due to COVID-19 41 years old our days are filled with morbid grotesque harsh life-threatening trauma we carry on expecting positive gains but are stepped on trounced pummeled by nuts Russian flavor sordid incompetence as if they are willing to use these present circumstances as an opportunistic culling event killing off those undesirable as most have survived this Christmas without even crumbs to give to Tiny Tim as homelessness hunger starvation pick off family after family Moscow Mitch still plays his favorite game Russian roulette with for our lives in this moment of reflection could their not have been another way instead of the current now inescapable in lethality. Yes, there was but greed power wealth posed the existential corruption now dominating our tentative futures. Bravo to all the creeps out there caused this Bravo you indiscreet murderous assassins way to go you f"***** nuts.

So I've been a thinkin' it's about time to do somethin' about time and how it can help manage our successful futures man has since the Stone Age been trying to tame his environment bumbling through effort after imperfect effort using anything found on the ground in trees underground in caves underwater or whatever falls outta the sky we continue to strive for human perfection Trumpdemic should be the slap in the face the wakeup call we have not been anywhere near redeeming now our time lives are slip sliding away we need to take control mastery of time improves potentials for timely viability. Time can be altered large stars and planets bend spacetime fabric of gravity. This flexing causes smaller objects to orbit the larger tilting or not in the revolution around time here increases and decreases now imagine there is a lot of this kind of planetary space bending twisting and flexing some of which can take the shape of funnel-like paths extending light years without reshaping unless collisions black holes are reinforcing some swallowing others these funnel-like paths are wormholes existent due to astrophysical quantum mechanics waiting for our arrival in some circumstances that can be man generated gravity can be focused to a singularity where time stands still at that moment a gravimetric frequency variable interaction modulation can put a Quantum ship in extra linear or cause you to transmigrate from linear to nonlinear time adjacent to our time but not influenced by our time thus at this moment you have crossed boundaries and thresholds now Quantum navigating in another time and space thus you have achieved time travel for every micromini-second of your movement could place you at the Big Bang or 300 years into an uninhabited future this would take instrument calibrations. When we have gained Metacognition of time we can improve our human condition through quality time, time spent with friends, time with family, time for recreation, time for self-improvement, time for this time for that time to get hit with a wiffle ball bat. Hey! What time is it really? What Time Is It?

Ok, I've heard enough so many doctors reporters nurses front liners politicians say in response to a question Are you able to see the government helping at this time of desperate need White House is radio silent POTUS just lying dog faced cheat lying still poddy mouth about winning Ga Arz PA MI all bald face grift right in front of cameras 45 minutes of the most twisted cows ass smelling lies POTUS if proud of nothing else can take a victory lap in the fat person cart most lies of any public servant in any country on earth even outdid Kim Jung illin pussy ass Putin China Saudi Arabian prince most lies in history for any servant of the people of all time. Comments are Trumpdemic behavior is mind boggling shocking panicked deluded biased desperate cynical caustic volatile fanatical tyrannical edgy. Are they kidding? Did they really expect different? If so, why? He has always acted like an ostrich with his head up his own ass now a lame quack whack duck his wide load big root asssssss is in all our faces. Mother****** is ass out.

"I snapped these two pictures of rare flying life forms or (RFLs).
I have 1200 more photos like these. Aliens or not Aliens?
You decide."